T0166876

VISION FOR
A NATION

RETHINKING INDIA 1

VISION FOR
A NATION:
PATHS AND
PERSPECTIVES

EDITED BY
AAKASH SINGH RATHORE
ASHIS NANDY

VINTAGE
An imprint of Penguin Random House

VINTAGE

USA | Canada | UK | Ireland | Australia
New Zealand | India | South Africa | China

Vintage is part of the Penguin Random House group of companies
whose addresses can be found at global.penguinrandomhouse.com

Published by Penguin Random House India Pvt. Ltd
7th Floor, Infinity Tower C, DLF Cyber City,
Gurgaon 122 002, Haryana, India

First published in Vintage by Penguin Random House India 2019

ISBN 9780670092949

Typeset in Bembo Std by Manipal Technologies Limited, Manipal
Printed at Replika Press Pvt. Ltd, India

www.penguin.co.in

Contents

Series Editors' Note

Psychologists tell us that the only *true* enemies we have are the faces looking back at us in the mirror. Today, we in India need to take a long, hard look at ourselves in the mirror. With either actual or looming crises in every branch of government, at every level, be it centre, state or local; with nearly every institution failing; with unemployment at historically high rates; with an ecosystem ready to implode; with a healthcare system in shambles; with an education system on the brink of collapse; with gender, caste and class inequities unabating; with civil society increasingly characterized by exclusion, intolerance and violence; with our own minorities living in fear; our hundreds of millions of fellow citizens in penury; and with few prospects for the innumerable youth of this nation in the face of all these increasingly intractable problems, the reflection is not sightly. Our true enemies are not external to us, not Pakistani terrorists or Bangladeshi migrants, but our own selves: our own lack of imagination, communication, cooperation and dedication towards achieving the India of our destiny and dreams.

Our Constitution, as the preamble so eloquently attests, was founded upon the fundamental values of the dignity of the individual and the unity of the nation, envisioned in relation to a radically egalitarian justice. These bedrock ideas, though perhaps especially pioneered by the likes of Jawaharlal Nehru, B.R. Ambedkar, M.K. Gandhi, Maulana Azad, Sardar Patel, Sarojini Naidu, Jagjivan Ram, R. Amrit Kaur, Rammanohar Lohia and others, had emerged as a broad consensus among the many founders of this nation, cutting across divergent social and political ideologies. Giving shape to that vision, the architects of modern India strived to ensure that each one of us is accorded equal opportunities to live with dignity and security, has equitable access to a better life, and is an equal partner in this nation's growth.

Yet, today we find these most basic constitutional principles under attack. Nearly all the public institutions that were originally created in order to fight against dominance and subservience are in the process of subversion, creating new hierarchies instead of dismantling them, generating inequities instead of ameliorating them. Government policy merely pays lip service to egalitarian considerations, while the actual administration of 'justice' and implementation of laws are in fact perpetuating precisely the opposite: illegality, criminality, corruption, bias, nepotism and injustice of every conceivable stripe. And the rapid rise of social intolerance and manifold exclusions (along the lines of gender, caste, religion, etc.) effectively whittle down and even sabotage an inclusive conception of citizenship, polity and nation.

In spite of these and all the other unmentioned but equally serious challenges posed at this moment, there are in fact new sites for sociopolitical assertion re-emerging. There are new calls arising for the reinstatement of the letter and spirit of our Constitution, not just *normatively* (where we battle things out ideologically) but also *practically* (the battle at the level of policy articulation and implementation). These calls are not simply partisan, nor are they exclusionary or zero-sum. They witness the wide participation of youth, women, the historically disadvantaged in the process of finding a new voice, minorities, members of majority communities, and progressive individuals all joining hands in solidarity.

We at the Samruddha Bharat Foundation proudly count ourselves among them. The Foundation's very raison d'être has been to take serious cognizance of India's present and future challenges, and to rise to them. Over the past two years, we have constituted numerous working groups to critically rethink social, economic and political paradigms to encourage a transformative spirit in India's polity. Over 400 of India's foremost academics, activists, professionals and policymakers across party lines have constructively engaged in this process. We have organized and assembled inputs from jan sunwais (public hearings) and jan manches (public platforms) that we conducted across several states, and discussed and debated these ideas with leaders of fourteen progressive political parties, in an effort to set benchmarks for a future common minimum programme. The overarching idea has been to try to breathe new life and spirit into the cold and self-serving logic of political and administrative processes, linking them to and informing them by grass-roots realities, fact-based research and social experience, and actionable social-scientific knowledge. And to do all of this with harmony and heart, with sincere emotion and national feeling.

In order to further disseminate these ideas, both to kick-start a national dialogue and to further build a consensus on them, we are bringing out this set of fourteen volumes highlighting innovative ideas that seek to deepen and further the promise of India. This is not an academic exercise; we do not merely spotlight structural problems, but also propose disruptive solutions to each of the pressing challenges that we collectively face. All the essays, though authored by top academics, technocrats, activists, intellectuals and so on, have been written purposively to be accessible to a general audience, whose creative imagination we aim to spark and whose critical feedback we intend to harness, leveraging it to further our common goals.

The inaugural volume has been specifically dedicated to our norms, to serve as a fresh reminder of our shared and shareable overlapping values and principles, collective heritage and resources. Titled *Vision for a Nation: Paths and Perspectives*, it champions a plural, inclusive, just, equitable and prosperous India, and is committed to individual dignity, which is the foundation of the unity and vibrancy of the nation.

The thirteen volumes that follow turn from the normative to the concrete. From addressing the problems faced by diverse communities—Adivasis, Dalit-Bahujans, Other Backward Classes (OBCs)—as well as women and minorities, to articulating the challenges that we face with respect to jobs and unemployment, urbanization, healthcare and a rigged economy, to scrutinizing our higher education system or institutions more broadly, each volume details some ten specific policy solutions promising to systemically treat the issue(s), transforming the problem at a lasting *structural* level, not just a superficial one. These innovative and disruptive policy solutions flow from the authors' research, knowledge and experience, but they are especially characterized by their unflinching commitment to our collective normative understanding of who we can and ought to be.

What the individual volumes aim to offer, then, are navigable road maps for how we may begin to overcome the many specific challenges that we face, guiding us towards new ways of working cooperatively to rise above our differences, heal the wounds in our communities, recalibrate our modes of governance, and revitalize our institutions. Cumulatively, however, they achieve something of even greater synergy, greater import: they reconstruct that India of our imagination, of our aspirations, the India reflected in the constitutional preamble that we all surely want to be a part of.

Let us put aside that depiction of a mirror with an enemy staring back at us. Instead, together, we help to construct a whole new set of images. One where you may look at your nation and see your individual identity and dignity reflected in it, and when you look within your individual self, you may find the pride of your nation residing there.

Aakash Singh Rathore, Mridula Mukherjee, Pushparaj Deshpande and Syeda Hameed

Introduction

Aakash Singh Rathore and Ashis Nandy

For about three millennia, Indic civilization has protected and nurtured two cardinal principles—self-reflection and diversity. Self-reflection not in the narrow sense that leads to an individual's self-realization, but in the grander sense of self-transcendence as a source of genuine creativity, and its humble adjunct—self-criticism as a means of social renewal.

As for diversity, Indic civilization does not demand mere tolerance of diversity. It demands the celebration of diversity. Not only because diversity overlies unity, as we often say, but because diversity is natural, sameness is not. Biologists claim that diversity is the first principle of life, whereas sameness—as evolutionary biology attests—can kill. The principle of diversity has turned our entire country into a contact zone, which some psychologists identify as a major source of social, cultural and intellectual creativity.

The clue to our cultural survival and creativity lies in these two principles. Alas, both are under attack today. Resisting this attack and refusing to jump onto the bandwagons of petty despots—local, regional or global—is our duty. We are optimistic enough to believe that, while regimes come and go and states can sometimes forget their heritage, civilizations have a way of humbling the mightiest of rulers.

Ideas of India

In his audacious book, *Why India Is Not a Great Power (Yet)*, Bharat Karnad explores the idea of conceiving of an India that would have:

> a driving vision, an outward thrusting nature backed by strong conviction and sense of national destiny and matching purpose, an inclination to establish distant presence and define national interests within the widest possible geographic ambit, the confidence to protect and further those interests with proactive foreign and military policies, and the willingness to use coercion and force in support of national interests complemented by imaginative projection and use of both soft power and hard power to expansively mark its presence in the external realm.[1]

This is *an* idea of India. One amongst innumerable alternative visions, rival conceptions, and yet still ensconced firmly within the fundamental idea (*ideas*) of India established in our Constitution. We take it for granted that within any vision for the nation, competing ideas of India must battle it out within the arena delineated by the Constitution; this is the very meaning of the term 'India' within a phrase such as 'Rethinking India', for we are rethinking the potentialities available to us to be imagined in line with the vast— but not infinite!—horizon of our founding document.

Ideas of India are thus decidedly not ideas of *Indias*. There are indeed regions, peoples, persons and ideologies all defiant of the sovereignty that the Constitution grants to India over all its territories; opposed to the Indian state's ostensible monopoly over violence; rejecting the constitutional idea (again, *ideas*) of India as such—terrorists, separatists, anarchists, fascists; some arguably justified, others clearly pathological. Here, however, the questions will not spiral around whether India is sovereign or not; we credit the sovereignty claimed in the constitutional preamble. Rather, we query what that sovereignty is and does, what it ought to mean and effect, and probe the chasm between its realities and possibilities.

But with the state granted, we inevitably face the bogey of the nation.

Indians of No Nation

During an early face-to-face encounter between Gandhi and Dr Ambedkar, it is reported that the latter remarked, 'Gandhiji, I have no homeland.' Ambedkar's autobiographical fragment, *Waiting for a Visa*,[2] gives us hints about how to understand this claim. Reflect for a moment on that autobiography's title: exactly which visa is Dr Ambedkar waiting for?

A visa, of course, is an official document permitting a person to cross borders and freely travel in or through a foreign country. In this case, it appears that the 'foreign' country must be India—Ambedkar is treated as alien here; is this a nation denied to him?

Like an outsider, Ambedkar is hindered all along the way from entering the society freely, from finding accommodation for overnight stays, from travelling without harm or obstruction. Indeed, his life story reveals that a former 'untouchable' seems to require some sort of visa, granted as a privilege and not a right, in order to be able to enter Indian social life on an equal footing with bona fide nationals.

The visa for which Dr Ambedkar remained forever in waiting is in a sense the same visa that had been denied to Rohith Vemula,[3] to Dr Payal Tadvi,[4] and to millions of others for whom their tragic stories resonate so viscerally. These tragic stories are not the ones that we believe characterize the rich potentialities inherent in our civilizational past; these tragic stories are not the ones we believe should continue to re-emerge in our nation's future—*they* are what should be alien to our vision for a nation.

So, who is in and who is out, and who gets to decide? By which precise criterion do we distinguish the bona fide national from the outsider, or those on the margins forever at risk of falling outside, the Dalit-Bahujan, the Muslim, the Adivasi, the queer, the supposed anti-national? This is a thorny knot that we have been unable to bloodlessly untangle in these seventy years of the republic.

Competing Nations—Love and Hate

Building upon the academic work of Benedict Anderson, Ernest Gellner and Anthony Smith, scholars continue to debate the origins and nature of the nation and nationalism—is it primordial with all political formations, or is it peculiarly modern? Does it function as a benefic cohesive force, or is it more a system of social control that permits elites to retain power? Decades prior to these debates, India had its own vibrant rival conceptions of the nature of the nation, forwarded by leading intellectual political practitioners from across the full breadth of the political spectrum, from anarchist to totalitarian.

We have long heard encomiums to the ideas of Gandhi or Nehru on the nation, and, given the unfulfilled promise of either, the last decade has rightfully elicited increased attention to the more inclusive and egalitarian vision of the likes of Ambedkar. But there are other authors and positions that the leading intelligentsia have tended to altogether ignore, or only evoked in order to ridicule. Ironically, however, it is apparently these academically marginalized and only partially interrogated conceptions of the nation that seem to grab and hold the political imagination of a majority of our fellow citizenry. It is time, in order to more adequately comprehend ourselves, that we think through and evaluate these ideas of the Indian and of the nation as well.

We could cite the example of Deen Dayal Upadhyaya here. Upadhyaya obviously has his champions on the right, but he has never been absolutely assimilated into the saffron nationalist pantheon where the likes of V.D. Savarkar and M.S. Golwalkar rest. According to Upadhyaya, 'When a group of persons lives with a goal, an ideal, a mission, and looks upon a particular piece of land as motherland, this group constitutes a nation.'[5] Hence, Upadhyaya is anchoring participation in the nation within the realm of ideas. While still largely reactionary, Upadhyaya's conception affords a certain flexibility with respect to national inclusion that is unavailable to mainstream nationalist thought, which grounds membership in the nation in exclusionary categories like ethnicity, religion and language.

In our own day, it is not territory and ideas that constitute the national bond between us. It does not even seem to be basic law, constitutional values or an inclination towards social security that pervade our cultural and political climate. As far as politics goes, classical concerns like rights and freedoms, federalism and democratic procedure have been all but abandoned to a civil (or some say uncivil) society largely characterized by intolerance and violence. People, ordinary Indians, are losing their lives on account of exclusionary categories like caste and religion. Every such tragic event, from individual suicide to mass pogrom, makes us wonder anew: will we never be able to achieve an overlapping consensus on inclusive national belonging, on being legitimately Indian?

Hatred is hot; it rallies crowds, and it tends to motivate more people more passionately than love and other such positive, but colder, concepts. Similarly, religion rallies more vehemence, and weaponizable obedience, than secularism ever will. Just the same, nationalism is hotter than constitutional patriotism, which is a much colder notion. The true challenge that faces us is this heat, this passion, emotion, which always falls naturally towards the right. We thus find ourselves fighting against the currents of natural passions when we seek to ignite mass support behind inclusive constitutional ideas as opposed to exclusive ethno-nationalist ones.

Can cold constitutional values such as fraternity, secularism and liberty ever quell the rage that hatred and nationalism have fomented on the streets, and chill this propensity towards violence?

Love, for example, even tolerant inclusion, is extremely difficult to vernacularize. And yet we have no alternative other than vernacularizing our basic constitutional values, of championing *sadbhavana* (goodwill), ahimsa, and a related basket of concepts that may contain more heat, more passion. It is a tall order to make fraternity and love politically organic, but inclusive concepts—ideological and not ethno-racial—must occupy the mental and spiritual space currently monopolized by exclusive ones.

G.N. Devy, in 'Epic, Narrative and Lyric Ideas of India', speaks at length of the centrality of love and compassion to the idea of India, while elaborating on various modalities of time and expression (epic, narrative and lyric) that have been part of Indic civilization for millennia. We are all familiar with exemplars of these genres: the Mahabharata, which represents the epic imagination of Indic civilization; the edicts of Ashoka, which characterize the narrative imagination; while the lyric imagination of India is apparent in Kalidasa's play, *Abhignana Shakuntala*. What is particularly fascinating in all of this is the manner in which our emotive orientations get unearthed through these various representations of our imagination.

Devy aims to reveal that the limited political imagination of current times indicates an abrupt break from our long civilizational trajectory, which decidedly favours compassion over hatred. The autocratic present squeezes our wide, multifaceted and loquacious national imagination, and makes those who represent our thoughts, moods and feelings in words pay the ultimate price. He poignantly lists the names of many persons who have been killed for putting thought into word.

Contrary to this manifestation of hate, Devy spends some time delving into our deeper civilizational commitment to love: between humans and nature, between man and god, between individuals and society, and one's relation with one's own self. He suggests that an all-pervasive love captures the essential teaching of archetypes of our nation, from the Buddha (*karuna*) to Mira to Gandhi (ahimsa).

Without reclaiming and disseminating these ideas, we will continue to be swept away by the exclusivistic sense of the nation, which we, in our fear and weakness, are permitting to define who gets to be a bona fide Indian, always with tragic consequences.

Reimagining our Communities

In *Imagined Communities*, Anderson, despite his multifaceted critique of nationalism, grants it the potentiality to project a utopian ideal that can bring peoples together: 'regardless of the actual inequality and exploitation that may prevail in each, the nation is always conceived as a deep, horizontal comradeship. Ultimately it is this fraternity that makes it possible, over the past two centuries, for so many millions of people, not so much to kill, as willingly to die for such limited imaginings.'[6] In a certain sense, Anderson's alarm over nationalism concerns more the content of it than the concept of it. That is, the tendency—especially true in India—is to pack the content of national belonging with exclusivist rather than inclusivist notions. Is it possible to retain the hot rubric of nation as a rallying concept but fill its content with the colder constitutional liberal and inclusive values?

Generally, liberal-minded and left-leaning scholars posit that constitutional patriotism alone can adequately promote the interests of everyone. Twenty-first-century elections around the globe, and within India for certain, seem to belie that claim. Constitutional patriotism is a modern concept anchored in the salience of the nation-state, offering the sugar-substitute of state-nation. What is sought is to imitate the affective capacity of the exclusivist orientation of nationalism with an equally affective enthusiasm for the state. The problem is, however, that it seems to depend upon imaginings as ahistorical and fuzzy as nationalism itself.

For example, in *The Discovery of India*,[7] Jawaharlal Nehru suggests that India was a nation in the making throughout the annals of history despite the fact that there was no such political entity as India before the Constitution. In other words, the secular and liberal values instantiated in the Constitution were constructed as valuable and viable in terms of a hoary—but indeed historically ambiguous—cultural legacy. In this way, Nehru himself took recourse to classic tropes of nationalism, evoking elements of race, territory, history, culture and so on, in order to stabilize his alternative to nationalism.

Ever since Savarkar's *Hindutva: Who Is a Hindu*,[8] which was reiterated and perversely martialized in Golwalkar's *We or Our Nationhood Defined*,[9] the saffron sense of nationalism has had a peculiarly modern, nineteenth-century character, feigning to resurrect tradition in five specific categories: language (on the one hand the sacralization of Sanskrit, on the other hand the imposition of Hindi), ethnicity/race (hence all the fuss and controversy surrounding the Aryan hypothesis), religion (the construction of a muscular Hinduism with the Gita as its holy book and Advaita Vedanta as its theology), territory and culture.

Hence their call for 'Hindi, Hindu, Hindustan'!

As Shashi Tharoor points out in his essay 'A Land of Belonging', Indian nationalism cannot rightly be based on these indices. Not on language, since our Constitution recognizes twenty-three official languages. Not on ethnicity, since Indians are empirically diverse in racial types. Indeed, Tharoor points out that many Indians (Punjabis and Bengalis, in particular) have more ethnically in common with foreigners (that is, Pakistanis and Bangladeshis, respectively) than they do with many of their compatriots, such as Poonawallas and Bangaloreans.

Not even on the trigger category of religion, because India is home to nearly every religion known to humankind, many of these flourishing in India prior to their arrival in Europe, such as Christianity itself. The category of territory also fails: the geography of the subcontinent, with the mountains and seas forming its natural borders, was subverted by Partition in 1947; moreover, by law, anyone with a grandparent born in pre-Partition India, which falls beyond the territorial boundaries of India today, remains eligible for citizenship.

For all these reasons, Indian nationalism cannot be sensibly conceived within the confines of the saffron nationalist categories.

For Tharoor, the idea of India, rather, is our nation as 'ever-ever land', emerging from ancient civilizations, united by shared histories, sustained by the plural character of its democracy. This is the idea that represents the soul of the Indian nation, not conformity to and hegemony of one thought or practice, but productive diversity carried forward through its constitutional promise.

The deep and long-lasting pluralism in India that Tharoor and Devy have both evoked is a fact. But the question that remains is whether it is also of value. This is Neera Chandhoke's focus in her essay entitled 'Secularism: Central to a Democratic Nation', where she takes up a robust defence of normative pluralism, while explaining the centrality of secularism to democracy. As Chandhoke argues, the oft-forwarded binary of secularism versus religion is false; the true opposite of secularism is communalism, and the inevitable logic of communalism in an agonistic social world is violence.

For Chandhoke, secularism is a thin, strictly procedural concept that is essential for the functioning of plural democracies. And if secularism is procedural, or operative within the domain of the state, then its social corollary is what we refer to as tolerance. Tolerance as a social virtue fortifies our civil society against explosions of violence. There is thus an urgency for us to understand the proper place of secularism in India, and the daily news of violence erupting across India lends credibility to Chandhoke's claims. For she finds a direct correlation between the decline in adherence to secularism today and the increase in violence against religious minorities. Thus, she seeks to breathe new life into secularism, but at the same time clarify that the concept is a thin and functional one, representing equality between religious groups, not a substantive one to be overburdened with the task of curing all of our social and political ills.

And though thin, it remains essential: secularism is a precondition for the viability of a plural democracy. As long as we remain committed to democracy where pluralism is a fact, we must operationalize secularism, or equality between religions, and as long as we value pluralism, we must maintain a commitment to secularism. To be sure, in the absence of pluralism, or in the absence of democracy, secularism may be discarded, but if pluralism or democracy is extant, then we are more or less choosing between secularism and violence.

Chandhoke's essay elegantly covers a great deal of terrain, and explains much about Indian realities. The only part that remains unexplained, because it remains entirely up to us, is what it is that we will do next. Shall we opt for the peaceful coexistence sought as far back in Indian practices and traditions as the *Shanti Parva* of the Mahabharata, or instead for the communal violence that always lies ready and waiting as human nature's baser instinct, standing by as the cheap and easy option?

Then What Lies Ahead?

What does the future of India look like—what ought it to look like? Can we share a broad-based consensus rooted in our expansive constitutional values? Or will the cheap seduction of saffron nationalism continue to erode our commitment to individual dignity as the necessary condition for the unity of the nation?

It is a truism that India enjoys (or should we still say 'suffers from'?) enormous variation in social, ethnic, religious, linguistic, cultural and historical realities. The challenge, here, is whether it is possible to transform this fact of pluralism into a value that is appreciated on the ground, appreciated not amongst like-minded progressives such as ourselves, but by everyday people, by the rightward leaning, by the youth. Nationalism *of some sort* seems our only available option for promoting solidarity out of this variegation.

And what about the content of these conceptions of the nation and nationalism—which ideas of India would be the ideas that we champion? Let's think for a moment towards the future: what is the legacy that we would wish to leave behind, what kind of India should we bequeath to the future generations? We ought to look beyond the present march of irrationality and focus on thinking long-term. But what of the youth now? It is often said of the youth in India today that they have become alienated from our founding values, that they prefer efficiency and opportunity to democratic freedom; indeed, it is suggested that the youth today would gladly opt for a Chinese model where economic prosperity is readily available over Indian democracy. However that be, we must not abandon these youth or segments of the middle-class who may share this preference for prosperity over liberal, foundational freedoms. We must win them over.

Human nature craves certitudes. Lack of certitudes forces people to fall back upon prejudices. We have enjoyed a galaxy of certitudes in the past: the nation-state, development, secularism, democracy and so on. Whereas these concepts have been hijacked by regressive forces, they are not ideas that we can abandon. Rather, we must rearticulate these fundamental values in terms accessible to common people, average citizenry, and especially to the youth.

Progressives have lost hold of these concepts. They need to be reclaimed, rearticulated, diffused on the ground level. We cannot give them up as our nation is founded upon them. But we can reinvigorate them for the current time. And we must. We need a revitalized vision for our nation.

Vision for a Nation: Paths and Perspectives

In what follows, several of India's leading thinkers and activists present a collection of paths and perspectives forward.

In his essay 'Indian Nationalism versus Hindutva Nationalism', Sitaram Yechury, no stranger to seeking common ground and forging alliances, articulates actions we need to take in order to defeat the current aggressive efforts to transform the plural and democratic vision of India into a rabidly intolerant, even fascistic Hindutva Rashtra, aiming to impose the homogeneity of 'Hindi, Hindu, Hindustan' upon the diverse character of our nation. For Yechury, the battle of ideas, such as the ideas of India, can only be meaningfully won if it is materialized, made a social, economic and political reality, rather than being only noble thoughts and words. To achieve this end, Yechury outlines the imperative steps:

> The drawing in of the exploited majority of rural India; the drawing in of the socially oppressed people, especially those who continue to be subjected to obnoxious caste-based oppression and atrocities; the drawing in of the numerous linguistic nationalities; the drawing in of the multireligious Indian population, and above all, the drawing in of all Indians in an inclusive path of economic and social justice, constituting the core of the inclusionary 'idea of India', remains an unfulfilled agenda. The struggles for realizing these incomplete tasks define the essential agenda.

Widening the invitation to collaborate by extending it even to Narendra Modi himself, S.Y. Quraishi—in his essay entitled 'From the Largest Democracy to the Greatest Democracy'—suggests that Prime Minister Modi's slogan 'Sabka saath, sabka vikas, sabka vishwas' (with/for the support, development, and trust of everyone) is perfectly consistent with the progressive vision of the architects of India, who sought the equal opportunity of every Indian to live with dignity and security, of every Indian to live a better life as an equal partner in the nation's growth—all of this was enshrined in the Constitution.

But when the leaders of government enact policies and encourage practices that undermine the Constitution, debilitate the institutions created in order to implement its principles, and vilify and perpetrate violence against persons of specific castes, genders and communities, then what is meant by the 'sab' (everyone) in Modi's slogan? It is not the 'We, the people of India' who appear first in our Constitution, but some other We (could it be the 'We' of Golwalkar's book title?). 'Sab' must mean all of us, 'We, the people of India', and not just those of us of certain castes, genders and religions.

Quraishi sees 'We, the people' as a crucial resource, rather than as a liability, for continuing the past several decades of explosive growth. That means that the inclusivity of that growth is a precondition for its continuation. Income inequality now stands at its highest level in Indian history, with money accruing to the top 1 per cent instead of spreading fairly to all Indians. This is a hazard to the constitutional idea of India itself. Especially considering that we are the youngest nation on earth, without a robust economy that spreads growth, we will continue to perpetuate the sort of jobless growth that we have seen since the BJP took power, and waste the resource of our youthful population. Worse, it will metastasize into rampant unemployment, which is a failure of India's constitutional promise as well as a major security concern for all. For these reasons, Quraishi lists out specific reforms which would help to achieve the constitutional ideas—ideals—of India.

Syeda Hameed, in 'A Shared Past, an Uncertain Future', speaks poignantly about exactly this choice before us, about synergistic communities, where everyone is brought on board the project of realizing the constitutional vision of India, versus perpetuating hatred of differences, lynch mobs against individuals, and communal violence. Through a passionate first-person narrative, Hameed leads her readers into the social and spiritual milieu of another era altogether, what must seem like a dream to us now—it is the India of her dreams. In this fantasy, for it is no longer permitted to be our real history, Muslims celebrated the festivals of Sikhs, Hindus and others, and vice versa; people across communities could appreciate the poetry, literature, song, cuisine and overall cultures of India's religiously plural landscape. Hameed prizes and passionately evokes our syncretic vision of India, which was not only a constitutional mandate but also regarded as a true social reality for the future. That future has never come. Our political present seeks to ensure that such a social future is precluded. Now, unity means homogeneity and difference means danger. Hence the vilification of half of us Indians, the marginalization, the exclusion.

All this suggests that today, what we are carrying forth as the legacy from the period surrounding our 1947 Independence and emergence as a sovereign nation is not the Constitution, but the acrimonies and violence of our Partition.

Further interrogating the ideas of marginalization and exclusion, an irrepressible voice of Dalit-Bahujan self-understanding, Kancha Ilaiah Shepherd (in 'The Fate of Shudras in a Buffalo Nation') unfolds a passionate plea for the erstwhile Shudras (in today's parlance, the OBCs) to awaken from their false consciousness. Using primarily the motifs of spiritual subservience and stubborn refusal to embrace the progressive principles of the new social and economic world within which modern India finds itself placed, Shepherd exhorts the OBCs to focus on their education and on attaining mastery of the English language, as a catalyst towards their eventual realization that—to purloin the phrase from Marx—they have nothing to lose but their chains.

Which chains? The OBCs or Shudras constitute the largest social bloc in India, but the various numerous communities are isolated from each other and fail to cooperate in collective action beyond the local level. All the shifts in identity, fracturing into different sub-castes, has worsened the situation. This lack of collective feeling has pushed them further into the margins, despite their numbers and their crucial contributions to the social history and economic productivity of the nation. As a consequence, their development has been stunted, and they remain subject to the traditional casteist contempt that Manu's ideology and reactionary Hindu theology and praxis sanction. They continue to be denied access to priesthood, and despite this spiritual subservience, they continue to form the major vote bank for the very political parties that spiritually and ideologically suppress them. As Shepherd points out, 'Not a single Shudra leader was allowed to become the sarsanghchalak of the RSS [Rashtriya Swayamsevak Sangh], nor did the RSS fight for the priesthood rights of the Shudra Hindus.'

The large-scale false consciousness and easy manipulability of the erstwhile Shudras is depicted by Shepherd through two main types of examples. First is with respect to food culture, within which Shudra traditions are being systemically obliterated right before their very eyes through tropes that they cannot cope with or resist, thanks to their failure to have taken up education and their exclusion from spiritual autonomy. Second, and related to aspects of the first, is the example of Shudra women compelled to protest their own free access to temples—to protest, that is, against their own rights. This latter phenomenon resonates with B.R. Ambedkar's analysis of Brahminical patriarchy, a concept that Shepherd only hints at, but which Kalpana Kannabiran makes explicit.

In 'Feminist Futures and Ideas of Justice for India', Kalpana Kannabiran takes up the deeply aspirational nature of the Indian Constitution, and suggests that our pledge of fidelity to the Constitution is a commitment to incessant reawakenings—continuing to awaken to new realities wherein we are obligated to act so that the ideals of the preamble, such as liberty and dignity, can be realized.

Given that Indian society is fractured by caste, religion and patriarchal norms, including heteronormativity, and that the now waxing Hindu nationalism exacerbates and weaponizes these differences and tensions, a commitment to reawakening seems utopian. But there are examples and exemplars that give us hope. Kannabiran attempts to cull out aspects of the Supreme Court case *Navtej Singh Johar vs Union of India* (decriminalizing sexual relations between consenting adults) as one such exemplar, a case of what she, following Upendra Baxi, calls 'insurgent constitutionalism'. She thus uses *Johar* as a lens through which to examine feminist futures and questions of justice for the excluded and marginalized.

The importance of this judgment is further magnified within the larger setting of civil and political rights that are today imperilled due to right-wing Hindu majoritarianism, which is dismantling constitutional institutions at various levels of the Indian polity. Kannabiran thus focuses on the *Johar* case as exemplifying a constitutional commons—where stigma and violence are eschewed, and where ideas of liberty, equality and queer sororal fraternity find their binding force—that permits Ambedkar's call for constitutional morality to be heeded.

Navtej Singh Johar also speaks for himself, or, rather, speaks as a civil rights activist, yoga practitioner and Bharatanatyam dancer, but on behalf of all of us seeking to forge an alliance for progressive imaginings of the nation. In 'Imagining and Embodying the Nation', Johar introduces the notion of embodiment, which is so important to our everyday lived experience. Free and fluid movement of bodily expression is as fundamental as freedom of speech and expression as such, although we think less about it. Only in a liberal, plural society are we free to explore with our bodies as well as our minds—to be creative, challenging, transgressive, all the preconditions of vibrant art and cultural life. And the reverse side of this coin is crucial too: non-normative bodies, such as the disabled, can only be accommodated without stigma when we recognize how homogenous ideologies constantly discipline and control our bodies, and indeed our minds through our bodies, as Antiphon the Sophist had claimed long back:

> By law it has been laid down for the eyes what they should see and what they should not see; for the ears what they should hear and they should not hear; for the tongue what it should speak, and what it should not speak; for the hands what they should do and what they should not do . . . and for the mind what it should desire, and what it should not desire.[10]

Law controls our bodies and minds, regulates the possibilities of embodiment and imagination, and this law is made by the government. There is, then, much more at stake with an illiberal government than you might at first think.

Speaking on the side of imagination, Johar also points out the slow and steady closing of the myriad, diverse and rival philosophical traditions of India, which is leaving us with only one system that we must adhere to in order to be part of the nation:

> A very wide spectrum of plurality—valid schools of thought including the heterodox, orthodox, idealist and materialist, which offered a multitude of varied perspectives on primary concepts such as karma, ahimsa, atman, brahman, God, vegetarianism, agency, morality, purity are practically lost to us. Today, this plurality has all been morphed or erased out of our consciousness. Vedanta alone remains as the abiding and predominant school of valid thought in popular consciousness; in fact, it has almost become synonymous with Hinduism. Today, in effect, we are left with no other way, than just one, to be Hindu. We have not paid attention to, even overlooked and undermined, our own philosophies, and as a result we are left with one unified Hindu philosophy that offers a 'categorical' version of truth.

Partly for this reason, Pushparaj Deshpande sees our present-day political struggle as a struggle for truth, and for the recognition of who we can and ought to be—what he calls a 'battle for India's soul'. And though he refers to this as a battle, his aim is to transcend the current state of spectacle, or gladiatorial politics, and seek cooperative and compassionate progress, together.

One of the major hindrances of this cooperative progress is ideological rupture, not only laterally, across our increasingly polarized communities, but also generationally. So many of us like-minded progressives may speak of justice, liberty, equality, secularism, democracy, but of what value are these concepts to India's massive youth population? Are we championing dated concepts? Does the Constitution's preamble, which inspired India's generations until now, still resonate with the millennial multitude, which sees so many of the constitutional institutions, bodies and branches as corrupt and/or elite? As Deshpande suggests, India's youth are:

> angry at being *left out* (because of poor access to English education, to opportunities of employment, to power, and most of all, to the kind of life they see in popular culture and everyday life) and even angrier at being *held behind* (because of nepotism, corruption and supposedly unfair state patronage towards minorities and historically marginalized communities). Shockingly, they also fear that civil society organizations, non-governmental organizations, the intelligentsia and sections of the media are instruments of the elite deployed to maintain the status quo. Even though some of these notions are fuelled by atavistic prejudices that have no place in a civilized society, the bitter reality is that many Indians hold this elite responsible for their plight.

In expressing these anxieties and calling all of us forth to action, Deshpande seems right to call this a battle for India's soul.

Shashi Tharoor certainly agrees, as he has offered this prescient caution in his own essay:

> This is a battle for India's soul. All of us who believe in the liberal values embodied in our Constitution must strive to ensure that the ultimate winner must be the idea of India. Indians must remain faithful to our founding values of the twentieth century if we are to conquer the twenty-first.

*

We all seem to know these truths, these values, these principles, and we share them, even where we disagree on numerous particulars and policies, in a sort of overlapping consensus. But there is an intractable problem that still stares at us in the face: how do we communicate this vision, these ideas of India, to the youth of the nation? How can we help make the spirit of our constitutional preamble breathe life into the bodies, minds and souls of India's future generations?

In this volume, we present an alliance of like-minded voices and seek to evolve a consensual position that functions collectively as a positive counter-narrative to reclaim the centrality of the progressive, constitutional ideas of India, a deeply plural India, reinvigorated for use in our own day. We hope that you will help us in spreading these ideas with compassion.

Epic, Narrative and Lyric Ideas of India

G.N. Devy

The beginnings are many. Geological research places the formation of the Himalayas to a time fifty million years ago.[1] Genomic research has accepted that the spread of the original population in India was from the peninsular south to the west and north. Plant genetics has determined that agricultural practices began spreading from Iran to what is now India some nine thousand years before our time. Archaeology takes us back five millennia to trace the roots of our civilization. Linguistic and literary history have succeeded in tracking our path back to a period spanning four thousand years. History, based on verifiable evidence, has pieced together an India of the last twenty-seven hundred years. The dawn of Indian civilization thus has several beginnings.

Given the as yet only partially fulfilled quest to know who we are and where we came from, the picture of India prior to the last twenty-five hundred years has so far remained abundantly hazy and the topic of many inconclusive debates. These debates are such that no one side can be designated as being entirely ill-conceived. I shall, therefore, not get into the question of 'the beginning' of Indian civilization. Rather, I would like to propose that leaving that question perennially open is one of the foundations of

Indian civilization. What we have been as a civilization may get completely altered if we were to arrive at a hypothesis about the remote past that brooks no exception.

William Shakespeare's ability to remain amidst uncertainties was described by John Keats as 'negative capability',[2] a great compliment by a great poet. If one may use that phrase in our context, one can say that the foundations of the diverse philosophical schools, literary traditions, linguistic cultures, religious faiths and social practices are almost entirely based on this ability to remain unchallenged by uncertainties, a civilization's great negative capability. It is this quality that informs our attitude towards the object world—the universe of experience, cultural values and conceptual understanding of reality.

Civilizations, cultures and societies keep changing, slowly but definitely, from century to century, from era to era. And it would not be less than impudent to assume that our civilization has remained the same all through its long history. Yet, despite the transitions, Indian civilization shows a remarkable continuity. The Harappan 'lota'-shaped vase still continues to be in use in India though now it is made in stainless steel. The musical notes even today draw on what Sarangdev or Matanga had set as their basic matrix. The semantics of gestures that the *Natyashastra* of Bharata had described as their performance grammar continue to be effective. One may not be too far off the mark in assuming that a profound belief in the continuity of things marks our philosophy, thought, expression, social fabric and cultural forms. The village in India, despite the plunder and devastation it has had to face over the past centuries, has held on and not withered primarily because we believe that continuity is natural and constitutes an abiding law of history. It is probably for the same reason that despite having massive movements aimed at change from century to century, India has not experienced what can be described as a revolution.

Invariably, all of the images of India that have emerged within Indian traditions carry a clear mark of these two—a negative capability allowing a sense of ease with the idea of many beginnings, and faith in an interminable continuity. Without altering the two, India has been imagined in the past using terms such as an epic time, a relatively vast span of time; a narrative time, a long albeit manageable period, and also a lyric time involving some focused periods of history. The three different imaginations of India have their specific flavours and generic flaws, but they also have their unique mesmerizing powers and captivating idioms. Instances of all three genres can be found in different periods of our composite history.

Epic Imagination

The most widely known epic imagination of India to be found among ancient texts is embedded in the Mahabharata. One is not pointing to its structure as an epic but rather to its epical presentation of the human condition. The narrative imagination is to be found in the edicts of Ashoka, and the lyric imagination of India can be located in Kalidasa's play *Abhignana Shakuntala*. The Mahabharata depicts several generations and an epoch-making conflict, a breathtaking range of characters, and an amazing wealth of wisdom and information on life as it then was. Western epics follow an unwritten rule in their composition: they begin the action in medias res, in the middle of things. The Mahabharata refuses to identify any single act or event as the beginning of its narrative. *Adi Parva*, the opening book of the epic, takes us through so many different beginnings, from Shantanu's wanderings to Bhishma's accursed celibacy to stories in the life of mountains, rivers, ghosts and animals, that it is virtually impossible to say where the actual story begins. Similarly, several parvas after the conclusion of the war, and even the one about the mythical *svargarohan* (ascent to heaven), indicate that the ever-moving wheel of life knows no end. In fact, the Mahabharata makes the wheel in perpetual motion its central metaphor. For the Mahabharata, that movement is the essence of dharma.

The edicts of Ashoka could have presented him like an Alexander, an all-powerful sovereign. But they resist doing so. He is depicted as 'devanampriya', a human 'dear to the gods', because he is humble and ready to serve all. That he chose to make the wheel his primary emblem indicates his understanding of the idea of India. The Shakuntala story is a lyrical statement of the same imagination of India. The story begins at once in the dev-loka where Dushyant is fighting the menace of the rakshasas and in Kanva's ashram where young Shakuntala is growing up. It does not end, as would a romance play in any Western tradition, with the reunion of Dushyant and Shakuntala, after their tragic separation caused by a temporary lapse of memory. It continues well past that point and presents to us their young son, Bharat, whose name is accepted as one of the two names of our country by the Constitution.

There are similar instances of the idea of India in medieval literature, paintings, music, iconography and architecture. The iconography is marked by figures that apparently point to a limitless space, a space without a beginning or an end. The medieval poetry of saints and social reformers such as Kabir, Nanak, Mira and Tukaram speaks of detachment and *aparigraha*[3] (non-possession or non-accumulation) and also of humility and love. We see these ideas at work once again in the literature and thought over the last two centuries, in the poetry of Ghalib, Iqbal and Rabindranath, in the novels by Gopinath Mohanty, Shivaram Karanth, Thakazhi Sivasankara Pillai, and in the life and thought of Mahatma Gandhi. All of them exalt humility and humanity, detachment and aparigraha, nobility of soul and love, acceptance of life beyond origin, caste, religion, language, occupation, and the pursuit of truth and non-violence. The epic, narrative and lyric ideas of imagination of India is that of a society bound together through empathy, compassion, understanding and love. It is the celebration of tolerance as a positive virtue, non-aggression as dharma, and sacrifice in the interest of truth as heroism.

It is, of course, not an idea focusing entirely on the spiritual and moral. It also celebrates, with gusto, the pleasures of the senses that fairs and festivals, music, dance, the arts and crafts bring to us. It is an idea of India where togetherness of the spiritual and the sensory, of the diverse and the different, of nature and animal is a non-negotiable article of faith. Compassion and love are central to that idea of India, and hatred and violence are anathema to it. Let me add something more about love here.

Love, Truth and their Antonyms[4]

The word 'love' has forever excited the human imagination. In many ways it has moved countless individuals more profoundly than even hunger and fear of death might ever have done. Yet, love has not been an unchanging, eternal emotion, nor has it had exactly identical connotations across cultures and over different epochs in history. In our history, the relatively more open society of the early Vedic times subsequently turned ghettoized and morally rigid. Bold, courageous women as characterized in the Mahabharata were brought to suffocation within the inflexible frame of the caste code. The pre-Kalidasa Shakuntala could not resurface with all her wanton will in the poet's time, and the questing Savitri of the previous era was reduced in later centuries to the exemplar of wifely devotion. Despite the much-celebrated Radha and Mira of myth, history and legend, Indian women have had to suffer a near animal-like existence, caged within the typecast identities of wife or widow, denied expression and space to both show and experience love.

Over the last century and a half, social reformers in India have had to fight many battles in the long-drawn, still ongoing, struggle to establish love as a natural human emotion. Literature, theatre and cinema have made very significant contributions to lifting the status of love from a taboo to a totem. But the khap panchayats continue to exist, and caste and tribal distinctions still cling to us like an ominous shadow to a cursed body. Just as Dr Ambedkar's *Annihilation of Caste*[5] is a severe indictment of the idea and practice of caste, so is the heart-rending question of the tragic heroine of *Mughal-e-Azam* (1960), 'Pyar kiya to darna kya?' Love is no crime, why should one be so terrified? The question resonated in the minds of Indians like nothing else had. The courage and clarity with which it was asked made the movie a classic for all time. It was a reminder, though, that love is still illicit, it still needs to fight for the space it should take for granted.

One should add that love is not a sentiment defining the man–woman relationship alone. Love can be the foundation on which several other fundamental relations can be built. These include the relation between humans and nature, between man and god, between individuals and society and, of course, one's relation with one's own self. Such an all-pervasive love was at the heart of the life and teachings of the Buddha, Mira and Gandhi. This higher-category love is what the Buddha called karuna and Gandhi ahimsa. One way to understand the futuristic nature of the concept of love is to read it in terms of these near synonyms. The other is to look at it from the perspective of its antonym, hatred.

One of the critiques of modern Western rationality is that it led to not only science but also violence. And just as science held logic as its ultimate test of authenticity, violence held hatred as its core validation. Over the last hundred years, hatred has driven the Nazis to create the Holocaust, whites in South Africa to practise apartheid, communists to carry out frequent purges of opponents, nation after nation to wage destructive military conflicts on neighbouring nations, terrorists to make entirely innocent people victims of brutal attacks. In the name of ideology, faith, territory and race, all drawing legitimacy from stereotyping, hatred and excessive self-love, humans have earned the distinction of being the unique species engaged in systematically exterminating its own members.

Limitless greed should be added to hatred as a related antonym of love. It induces silent genocide, triggers involuntary mass migrations, results in the proliferation of ecologically destructive projects, and generates emotion that makes love an outcaste, a pariah in the imaginaries of the futures. Hatred-driven violence is more manifest in modern times, but it is not that the past ages were entirely free of it. It is quite an enigma that despite knowing the spiritually healing power of love and its great social dividends, love has been a constant loser in the arena of the lived lives of humans.

Truth is another such idea. We all speak in its name. Even wars are fought to defend this or that version of truth. Yet, it would be impossible to establish in any material or logical form what 'truth' really is. We think we have access to its comprehensive meaning, but when put to a test one realizes how elusive the idea called 'truth' is. Love belongs to this peculiar category of concepts. Perhaps, the most problematic among the concepts in this category is god. Innumerable individuals have made attempts throughout the ages to grasp the idea of 'god', to experience it through the sensory or mental agencies within the command of humans and to describe it. The results of their attempts have produced numerous schools of theology, but no ultimate and undisputed description or representation.

Given the nature of these concepts, they come to be seen as deeply interrelated or even as synonyms. Thus, it becomes both possible and necessary to maintain that truth is god or vice versa. Or beauty is love or vice versa. Since such is the nature of the concept 'love'—postulated for keeping phenomenological communities together, without having any 'knowable' meaning— our encounter with it is entirely 'ours'. To draw an analogy with the similar notion of god: every temple, statue, image, painting, photograph and depiction of god remains essentially our depiction rather than god herself or himself.

However, despite these lofty ideals embedded in the best expressions of our civilization, there have also been the contrary— violence, hatred, intolerance and falsehood—manifest at all times in our history. Orthodoxy and dogma, the violence surrounding caste discrimination, and the demeaning of women in Indian society too have been recurrent features of our history. These have continuously led to marginalization of castes, communities and women. When the Constitution was formed, it brought in the lofty ideals of India and made every effort to remove the shameful practices associated with it. It is important to understand the history, or rather the histories, of structured violence in India when looking at the recurrent emergence of socially violent ideas and intolerant dogmas.

Notions of Citizenship[6]

It is difficult to say whether orthodoxy, as well as its nemesis, dynamism, are characteristic mores of a given society or ideas that it receives and internalizes. We believe that normally any major shift in a society's material conditions will necessarily bring about a shift in all of the ideas that constitute its foundations. But history is full of examples showing social progression largely without a corresponding shift in foundational ideas. Post-war Europe offers a classic range of this mismatch. History also has examples where ideas have moved ahead and societies have lagged miserably behind. Various varieties of colonial modernity offer a wide-spectrum testimony to this kind of mismatch. Since social formations as well as the architecture of ideas are shaped by humans, both kinds of mismatch result in tragic consequences for large numbers. In our immediate context, citizenship is a case in point.

A quick view of its evolution tells us that 'citisein', the old French origin of the term, was used to refer to 'the inhabitants of a city or a town'. This in turn was based on the idea of a home as a mental image of close relations. 'Domus' was Latin for 'home' and 'domicilium' for 'dwelling'. This sense was later picked up by the language of law in European countries and the idea of home as a 'residence from which one had no intention to shift' gained stability. Well, until what British history describes as a 'hundred years of war', the idea of citizen and the idea of habitat held mutual correspondence. But the war had created a need for a steady number of soldiery, and the number of soldiers under the royal command clearly depended on the stability of revenue. That fiscal need led England and France to move from taxation on agricultural yield to taxation on farmland. Yields can vary, but the area of land under cultivation was relatively steady. With the change in tax law, the meaning of 'citizen' moved closer to landownership and tax-paying ability. That served well for Europe during the seventeenth and eighteenth centuries. But its implications for colonized India were not so during the nineteenth century.

The British colonial administrators in India noticed that a large part of the population was migratory in nature. Apart from the large-scale religious pilgrimages of sects, they noticed that communities were not really rooted to a single specific habitat. The colonial mind felt that if these did not have a predictable land relationship, bringing them under the tax regime would be difficult. Upon noticing this, the regime did everything to bring them under control and to change their nomadic habits so that they became sedentary in thought and act. On the sidelines of the wars, cessations of states, building roads and rail tracks, pressing the English language in law and education, the colonial administrators kept themselves overbusy isolating all of the non-sedentary communities.

The colonial administrators' inability to understand the cultural and economic practices of nomadic groups in India resulted in a profound sociological tragedy. An officer like William Henry Sleeman was especially appointed to keep a watch on these 'thugs'. Given his position of authority and his unmatched enthusiasm about hunting for anything nomadic, it was no surprise that the 'thugee' myth took root in a few decades. The dignity acquired by the stereotypes he had floated was evident in the Criminal Tribes Act (CTA) of 1871,[7] which had a sizeable list of communities designated as 'criminal'. It included the transgender 'Hizras', coin-making 'Meenas', stone mason 'Wodders' and horse-mounted trading 'Sansis'. Other communities were brought under the draconian provisions in subsequent versions of the CTA. A total of 190 communities, whose current population may be close to 110 million,[8] were subjected to the provisions, kept in reformatory prisoner colonies—appropriately called 'settlements'— and branded as criminals and used for unpaid labour on public purpose civil works. Even after the country rose to independence, the communities wrongly branded as 'criminal' continued to languish in their settlements with pathetically meagre access to civil rights. A large mass of our own working population had thus been turned into less than citizens. In 1952, they were 'denotified', the CTA was slightly amended and a Habitual Offenders Act (HOA) replaced it. The spirit of the HOA was ditto.

The point I am trying to make here is not that nothing much has been done for the Denotified Nomadic Tribes. That indeed is the case. I am trying to point to the continued process of restricting the meaning of the term 'citizen'. The Indian Constitution in its most idealistic sweep of vision proposes full citizenship status for all of us. However, in the working of the law and regulations, it has routinely been getting truncated. This needs no elaboration when we look at the plight of the communities that do not speak any of the scheduled languages as their mother tongues. The state has been uninterested in creating access to education for them in their own languages. So, their linguistic citizenship is compromised. Our courts do not have law interpreters for all. Those who fail to understand the intricacies of law courts automatically become legal non-citizens. Those who have bank accounts and Aadhaar cards have some degree of a genuine economic citizen status. Those who do not have them lose out on this account.

Orson Welles's film *Citizen Kane* (1941) is a frightening statement of isolation that surrounds the idea of the citizen at the heart of a society that looks at capital and media as real power. Neo-liberal economies have been fast turning very large sections of the society into less than citizens. Of course, this is a global phenomenon and to a large degree an irreversible one. Yet, its implication affects human beings in flesh and blood, with their hunger and pain, joys and dreams, not just some digital numbers printed in grey ink by a chip-driven printer. The process of excluding citizens, aided by the technologies that are turning them into mobs, has gained sharper blades due to the nationalistic jingoism and theocratic bigotry that are getting normalized fast. Coercive tax regimes too are helping in the replay of history.

In an ideal world, democracies are expected to enlarge and deepen the citizenship rights of every segment of the society. That is a marvellous idea, but our world has precariously veered away from the ideal. So much so that thinking other thoughts, saying other prayers, eating other food, dressing in another way, remembering other heroes and histories have come to be seen by the minions of the state as acts of 'sedition' or 'treason'. Globally, the state itself is asking for greater rights to snoop, whether it is in Turkey, Egypt, Russia, the USA or in our own country. There was a time when those who were frowned upon had some constitutional guarantees to help them. But society has changed and the idea of constitutional democracy has not kept pace with it.

A century and a half ago, Karl Marx described many types of social segments deprived of all citizenship rights by using the term 'the have-nots'. Ambedkar used the term 'Dalit'. How does one describe in our present context all of the classes being treated as less than citizens, a kind of second-class citizens? We can probably call them, for linguistic ease, 'the gastflects', the ones afflicted by the goods and services tax (GST), the prized trophy of the current dispensation. These include the ones who have no jobs and housing, no access to education and healthcare, no Aadhaar card, no legal remedy, no possibility of restructuring their farm loans, and no real say in forming governments. Add to these the victims of widespread intolerance and minority-baiting. Hubris and hegemony are in the air, and innocent citizens are facing increased discrimination.

A Tale of Two Memorials[9]

When historical narratives become semantic beggars, anecdotes help in lighting up the collective memory. Some years back, I was in Berlin. This was the post-perestroika, unified Berlin. As I was walking outside the grand buildings of the Humboldt University of Berlin, where Karl Marx had been a student a century and a half ago, I noticed a curious installation. This was just outside the university library. It was designed to take one by complete surprise and shock. On the pavement, as one walked, one suddenly saw a small cavity covered in glass. It was the size of a cellar or a bunker. Inside it, there was some light, but not enough to show at once what was inside. As one peered into the dimly lit chamber beneath the glass floor one noticed a single shelf of books with just one or two books on it. The inscription placed next to the glass surface read, 'This is the place where Adolf Hitler burnt books of many thinkers in May 1932 after dragging them out of the library.' The inscription brought home the brutality of the regime that took pride in attacking free thought. The installation was an apt statement for the tradition of Marx brutalized by Hitler.

A related anecdote that comes to my mind is about the Kasturba Gandhi memorial at the Aga Khan Palace in Pune. Kasturba Gandhi died here when she had been imprisoned along with Mahatma Gandhi and Mahadev Desai at the height of the Second World War and the Quit India movement. In September 2018, I had the privilege of hosting a large conference in Pune in which writers from eighty-seven countries participated. I thought it would be a good idea to bring the writers to the Kasturba memorial, and so I did. I had imagined that these writers from far-off countries would look at the place, take a few photographs and then would want to leave. To my surprise, they suggested that they would like to sit down on the ground and observe silence as a tribute to Gandhi and Kasturba. The genuine respect and love they inspire even among those who are complete strangers to their work and ideas is phenomenal.

Though Hitler was younger to Gandhi by some twenty years, the two can be seen as contemporaries dominating the world stage. It was approximately at the same time that Hitler burnt books and Gandhi defied the colonial salt law and chose to be jailed. It was the same time when Gandhi came up with his idea of 'civil disobedience' as a statement of one's moral courage in the face of injustice and Hitler started demanding 'complete obedience' towards the supreme leader. Hitler justified and promoted violence in every form; Gandhi devoted himself to preaching non-violence. Hitler made propaganda the basis of his continued right to dominate, Gandhi spoke of truth as the path towards freedom.

It is an irony of history that the world is celebrating the 150th year of Gandhi's birth, 2018–19, precisely when the tendencies for which Hitler was known have started characterizing rulers in many countries. Was Gandhi's idea of truth so fragile that the world would forsake it not so long after his death? The writers gathered in Pune brought home to me poignantly that Gandhi is still seen by the larger humanity, irrespective of one's nation, creed, language and race, as the prophet of freedom. He returns to people's thought wherever love, freedom and truth are assailed. The post-truth era in history will no doubt make him sound as relevant as he was in the times of colonialism and Hitler's festival of violence. No installation will make him look dated and embarrassing, not even the ridiculous official caricature of him only as a pair of glasses done to promote the pet ideas of those who were brought up despising him.

Denying Dissent[10]

Autocratic regimes, whether right or left, hostile to any kind of criticism, have invariably shown utter disregard for dissenting voices. Of course, this alone does not define such regimes, but it certainly is one of their definitive features. If we look at our own treatment of dissenting voices, we do not have much room for taking a morally superior stand. Though most of us may have happily forgotten that in recent times a number of journalists and writers were killed in our country, our report card is not free of bloodstains.

Here is a random list of those who were killed because they were working with words: (2014) Tarun Kumar Acharya, M.V.N. Shankar; (2015) Jagendra Singh, Sandeep Kothari, Sanjay Pathak, Hemant Yadav; (2016) Karun Misra, Rajdev Ranjan, Kishore Dave; (2017) Gauri Lankesh, Shantanu Bhowmik, Sudip Dutta Bhaumik; (2018) Navin Nischal, Shujaat Bukhari, Chandan Tiwari. The states in which these killings happened include Odisha, Andhra Pradesh, Madhya Pradesh, Uttar Pradesh, Bihar, Gujarat, Jharkhand, Karnataka, Tripura and Kashmir. This list would be much longer if one were to include the killings of rationalists such as Govind Pansare and M.M. Kalburgi. It would be almost unmanageably longer were one to add the names of political workers butchered.

The question here is not how they were killed or who killed them, it is why they were killed. And the timeless and well-known answer to this question is that they were saying something that was not convenient for the rulers, that their thoughts were seen as 'dangerous'. Sadly, none of the killings generated as much censure and public debate as they should have. Sadly, again, they were passed off as if they were ordinary murders requiring ordinary police inquiries that end in dusty files becoming dustier as the agony of the families of the victim keeps growing duller and fades one day in the forest of cynicism.

This has been by no means an Indian phenomenon alone. The situation in Russia, China, Turkey, Brazil, the east European countries and our neighbour Bangladesh has not been different. Even the USA, a country that firmly stood for the freedom of expression throughout the decades of the Cold War, has had its share when it comes to suppression of the media, and Mr Trump's presidency has made that into an art with excellence. Though the news of explosives dispatched to the CNN office last year did not find headlines in our media, it did send shivers down the spines of people in US media circles.

What is it in the world that has changed so radically in recent years? There is, of course, no easy answer, and one is too close to the current era to be able to comment with much objectivity. Yet, I venture to offer a comment since I cannot accept silencing of dissent and intellectual opposition through violence as acceptable in a civilized society. One rather obvious explanation for the growing intolerance in the world is that during the last three decades nation after nation has moved away from the distributive-economic model for elimination of inequalities, which a range of left-oriented regimes and welfare states traditionally held as sacred, to an inspirational-growth model that conservative political parties and right-oriented states have been promoting.

In this shift from left-oriented economic views to right-oriented ones, the people in these nations have also gradually gravitated towards the political right, which according to Adolf Hitler's classic—read infamous—formulation believes that 'society is like a woman who likes to be tamed and mastered by a strong and powerful leader'.[11] For the last several years, the era of the perceived 'strong and masterly' leader has started unfolding in most parts of the world, and with this clemency towards violence-prone political regimes, nations have started tolerating extreme right political parties.

The Parliamentary elections in Spain held last in early 2019 resulted in nearly one-tenth of the elected members being from the ultra right. On 27 April, the day that Italy has celebrated as its 'liberation day' since 1945, the Italian ultra right took out a parade in Milan with banners showing Benito Mussolini and saluted the banner. The parade and salutation were all in the typical fascist style. In Sweden, France, Germany, Spain, Italy and of course Austria, the rise of the ultra right during the last few years has further kindled the hopes of these elements. They forged an unholy alliance to fight the European Union elections. How Europe copes with the ultra right and manages to safeguard the legacy of democracy there is another matter. What matters for us in India is that we have not been able to give enough thought to negotiating the transition from our left economic orientation to the growing aspiration-based model of development without allowing anti-democratic sentiment to rule our heads and hearts.

Hegemony and Hubris[12]

States that consciously encourage creating societies that forget to produce a critique of the system generate what the ancient Latin described as 'hegemony'. The term refers to the nature of power, but in hegemonies such uncontested power becomes possible entirely out of the majority's self-approved willingness to promote the dominant ideas and perspectives. It is a somnambulant social condition under which vast numbers are ready to impose the will of the rulers on the less powerful in the society. Hegemony that the amoral, complaisant and unthinking majorities fuel results in a politico-psychological illness that the ancient Greeks called 'hubris' among the ruling order. It looks like pride, but is a lot more than an ordinary person's pride in things good. It makes the ruling order forget why they are where they are. Hubris shuns dialogue. It avoids questions. It leads the ruling order to generate deafening self-righteous rhetoric, and makes it entirely remorseless.

Hegemony induced by orders drunk on hubris also start showing these tendencies. Masses that were at least human even when they were mobs become lynch mobs. The incurable pride of the rulers combined with the large sections of citizenry ready to crawl in order to fulfil the whims and wishes of the rulers make the society a lynch mob society. It begins its mission by lynching memory. It proposes new versions of history in which the ruling order must be depicted as 'the first' with nothing before it of any consequence. If there are dissenters, they are placed under sharp assault by troll armies. If they continue to raise their voice, they are shown the gate as traitors. The Midas touch of any ruler heavy with hubris quickens the taste for violence among the people he rules.

When mobile phones keep attacking the memory and minds of the masses every minute, the people become mobs and start lynching everyone and everything that they think their rulers do not like.

Both hegemony and hubris have their peculiar histories. Since hegemony likes to ban questioning, the suppressed questions start returning in strange forms. They erupt naked from Una. They cry in agony from Unnao.[13] They come up in slogans on campuses and between the lines in press columns. And a pinch of salt lifted at Dandi can unsettle an empire. Silenced memory returns after every exile with renewed vigour.

The timeless imagination of India rooted in the idea of a civilization with many beginnings and no conclusive ending, which surfaced again and again despite its negation and brutalization by forces driven by violence and hatred, needs to be recovered in every possible form. This is a mission far larger than merely the political. It is an ethical mission and an aesthetic mission as well. When it is taken up and brought to culmination, all else shall return to what India has been over the millennia: a compassionate and tolerant civilization. The struggle shall never end and certainly is never to be given up.

A Land of Belonging[1]

Shashi Tharoor

At midnight on 15 August 1947, independent India was born as its first prime minister, Jawaharlal Nehru, proclaimed 'a tryst with destiny . . . a moment . . . .which comes but rarely in history, when we step out from the old to the new, when an age ends, and when the soul of a nation, long suppressed, finds utterance'.[2] With those words he launched India on a remarkable experiment in governance. Remarkable because it was happening at all. 'India,' Winston Churchill once barked, 'is merely a geographical expression. It is no more a single country than the Equator.'[3] Churchill was rarely right about India, but it is true that no other country in the world embraces the extraordinary mixture of ethnic groups, the profusion of mutually incomprehensible languages, the varieties of topography and climate, the diversity of religions and cultural practices, and the range of levels of economic development that India does.

And yet India, I have long argued, is more than the sum of its contradictions. It is a country held together, in the words of Nehru, 'by strong but invisible threads . . . a myth and an idea, a dream and a vision, and yet very real and present and pervasive'.[4]

Just thinking about India makes clear the immensity of the challenge of defining what the idea of India means. How can one approach this land of snow peaks and tropical jungles, with twenty-three major languages and 22,000 distinct 'dialects' (including some spoken by more people than Danish or Norwegian), inhabited in the second decade of the twenty-first century by more than a billion individuals of every ethnic extraction known to humanity? How does one come to terms with a country whose population is nearly 30 per cent illiterate but which has educated the world's second-largest pool of trained scientists and engineers, whose teeming cities overflow while two out of three Indians scratch out a living from the soil? What is the clue to understanding a country rife with despair and disrepair, which nonetheless moved a Mughal emperor to declaim, 'if on earth there be paradise of bliss, it is this, it is this, it is this . . .?'[5]

How does one gauge a culture which elevated non-violence to an effective moral principle, but whose freedom was born in blood and whose independence still soaks in it? How does one explain a land where peasant organizations and suspicious officials once attempted to close down Kentucky Fried Chicken as a threat to the nation, where a former prime minister once bitterly criticized the sale of Pepsi-Cola 'in a country where villagers don't have clean drinking water',[6] and which yet invents more sophisticated software for the planet's computer manufacturers than any other country in the world? How can one determine the future of an ageless civilization that was the birthplace of four major religions, a dozen different traditions of classical dance, eighty-five major political parties and 300 ways of cooking the potato?

Many Indias

The short answer is that it can't be done—at least not to everyone's satisfaction. Any truism about India can be immediately contradicted by another truism about India. It is often jokingly said that 'anything you can say about India, the opposite is also true'. The country's national motto, emblazoned on its governmental crest, is 'Satyameva Jayate' (Truth Alone Triumphs). The question remains, however: whose truth? It is a question to which there are at least a billion answers—if the last census hasn't undercounted us again.

But that sort of an answer is no answer at all, and so another answer to those questions has to be sought. And this may lie in a simple insight: the singular thing about India is that you can only speak of it in the plural. There are, as the hackneyed phrase goes, many Indias. Everything exists in countless variants. There is no single standard, no fixed stereotype, no one way. This pluralism is acknowledged in the way India arranges its own affairs: all groups, faiths, tastes and ideologies survive and contend for their place in the sun. At a time when most developing countries opted for authoritarian models of government to promote nation-building and to direct development, India chose to be a multiparty democracy. And despite many stresses and strains, including twenty-two months of autocratic rule during the 1975 Emergency, a multiparty democracy—freewheeling, rumbustious, corrupt and inefficient, perhaps, but nonetheless flourishing—India has remained.

One result is that India strikes many as maddening, chaotic, inefficient and seemingly unpurposeful as it muddles its way through the second decade of the twenty-first century. Another, though, is that India is not just a country, it is an adventure, one in which all avenues are open and everything is possible. 'India,' wrote the British historian E.P. Thompson,[7] 'is perhaps the most important country for the future of the world. All the convergent influences of the world run through this society. There is not a thought that is being thought in the West or East that is not active in some Indian mind.'

Just as well a Brit said that, and not an Indian! That Indian mind has been shaped by remarkably diverse forces: ancient Hindu tradition, myth and scripture; the impact of Islam and Christianity; and two centuries of British colonial rule. The result is unique.

Many observers have been astonished by India's survival as a pluralist state. But India could hardly have survived as anything else. Pluralism is a reality that emerges from the very nature of the country; it is a choice made inevitable by India's geography and reaffirmed by its history.

Pluralism and inclusiveness have long marked the idea of India. India's is a civilization that, over millennia, has offered refuge and, more importantly, religious and cultural freedom, to Jews, Parsis, several varieties of Christians, and of course Muslims. Jews came to Kerala centuries before Christ, with the destruction by the Babylonians of their First Temple, and they knew no persecution on Indian soil until the Portuguese arrived in the sixteenth century to inflict it. Christianity arrived on Indian soil with St Thomas the Apostle (Doubting Thomas), who came to the Kerala coast sometime before 52 CE and was welcomed on shore by a flute-playing Jewish girl. He made many converts, so there are Indians today whose ancestors were Christian well before any Europeans discovered Christianity.

In Kerala, where Islam came through traders, travellers and missionaries rather than by the sword, the Zamorin of Calicut was so impressed by the seafaring skills of this community that he issued a decree obliging each fisherman's family to bring up one son as a Muslim to man his all-Muslim navy! This is India, a land whose heritage of diversity means that in the Kolkata neighbourhood where I lived during my high school years, the wail of the muezzin calling the Islamic faithful to prayer routinely blends with the chant of mantras and the tinkling of bells at the local Shiva temple, accompanied by the Sikh gurudwara's reading of verses from the Guru Granth Sahib, with St Paul's Cathedral just round the corner.

So the first challenge is that we cannot generalize about India. One of the few generalizations that can safely be made about India is that nothing can be taken for granted about the country. Not even its name: for the word India comes from the Indus River, which flows in Pakistan. That anomaly is easily explained, for we know that Pakistan was hacked off the stooped shoulders of India by the departing British in 1947. (Yet each explanation breeds another anomaly. Pakistan was created as a homeland for India's Muslims, but—at least till very recently—there were more Muslims in India than in Pakistan.)

How, then, does one define the Indian idea?

This nebulous 'Idea of India'—though the phrase is Tagore's—is, in some form or another, arguably as old as antiquity itself. However, the idea of India as a nation based on a certain conception of human rights and citizenship, vigorously backed by due process of law and equality before law, is a relatively recent and strikingly modern idea.

The British like to point out, in moments of self-justifying exculpation, that it is their achievement, that they deserve credit for the political unity of India—indeed, that the very idea of 'India' as one entity (now three, but one during the British Raj) instead of multiple warring principalities and statelets is the unchallengeable contribution of British imperial rule. I have gone at length into this claim in my recent book *An Era of Darkness* (2016).[8]

A Vision of Unity

As I point out, it is difficult to refute that proposition except with a provable hypothesis: that throughout the history of the subcontinent, there has existed an impulsion for unity. This was manifest in the several kingdoms throughout Indian history that sought to extend their reach across all of the subcontinent: the Maurya (322–185 BCE), Gupta (at its peak, 320–550 CE) and Mughal (1526–1857 CE) empires, and to a lesser extent, the Vijayanagara kingdom in the Deccan (at its peak 1136–1565 CE) and the Maratha confederacy (1674–1818 CE). Every period of disorder throughout Indian history has been followed by a centralizing impulse, and had the British not been the first to take advantage of India's disorder with superior weaponry, it is entirely possible that an Indian ruler would have accomplished what the British did, and consolidated his rule over most of the subcontinent.

The same impulse is also manifest in Indians' vision of our own nation, as in the ancient epics the Mahabharata and the Ramayana, which reflect an Idea of India that twentieth-century nationalists would have recognized. The epics have acted as strong, yet sophisticated, threads of Indian culture that have woven together tribes, languages and peoples across the subcontinent, uniting them in their celebration of the same larger-than-life heroes and heroines whose stories were told in dozens of translations and variations, but always in the same spirit and meaning. The landscape the Pandavas saw in the Mahabharata (composed approximately in the period 400 BCE to 400 CE) was a pan-Indian landscape, for instance, as their travels throughout it demonstrated, and through their tale, Indians speaking hundreds of languages and thousands of dialects in all the places named in the epic enjoyed a civilizational unity. Lord Rama's journey through India and his epic battle against the demon-king of Lanka reflect the same national idea.

After all, India has enjoyed cultural and geographical unity throughout the ages, going back at least to Emperor Ashoka in the third century BCE. The vision of Indian unity was physically embodied by the Hindu sage Adi Shankara, who travelled from Kerala in the extreme south to Kashmir in the extreme north and from Dwarka in the west to Puri in the east, as far back as the seventh century after Christ, establishing temples in each of these places that endure to this day. Diana Eck's writings on India's sacred geography extensively delineate ancient ideas of a political unity mediated through ideas of sacredness. As Eck explains: 'Considering its long history, India has had but a few hours of political and administrative unity. Its unity as a nation, however, has been firmly constituted by the sacred geography it has held in common and revered: its mountains, forests, rivers, hilltop shrines . . . linked with the tracks of pilgrimage.'[9]

Nor was this oneness a purely 'Hindu' idea. The rest of the world saw India as one: Arabs, for instance, regarded the entire subcontinent as 'al-Hind' and all Indians as 'Hindi', whether they hailed from Punjab, Bengal or Kerala. The great nationalist Maulana Azad once remarked upon how, at the Haj, all Indians were considered by other Muslims to be from one land—all 'Hindis'—and regarded themselves as such. Surely such impulses, fulfilled in those distant times by emperors and sages, would with modern transport, communications and far-sighted leaders have translated themselves into political unity?

Counterfactuals are, of course, impossible to prove. One cannot assert, for instance, with any degree of certitude, events that did not in fact occur, nor name that centralizing figure who might have been India's Bismarck, Mazzini, Atatürk or Garibaldi in the absence of the British. But historical events find their own dramatis personae, and it is unreasonable to suggest that what happened everywhere else would not have happened in India. Counterfactuals are theoretical but facts are what they are. The facts point clearly to the dismantling of the pre-existing political institutions of India by the British, the fomenting of communal division, and systematic political discrimination with a view to maintaining and extending British domination.

In the years after their victory at the Battle of Plassey in 1757, the British astutely fomented cleavages among the Indian princes, and steadily consolidated their dominion through a policy of 'divide and rule' that came to be dubbed, after 1858, *divide et impera*. The sight of Hindu and Muslim soldiers rebelling together in 1857 and fighting side by side, willing to rally under the command of each other and pledge joint allegiance to the enfeebled Mughal monarch, alarmed the British, who did not take long to conclude that dividing the two groups and pitting them against one another was the most effective way to ensure the unchallenged continuance of Empire. As early as 1859, the then British governor of Bombay, Lord Elphinstone, advised London that, 'divide et impera was the old Roman maxim, and it should be ours'. The creation and perpetuation of Hindu–Muslim antagonism was the most significant accomplishment of British imperial policy: the project of divide et impera would reach its culmination in the horrors of Partition that eventually accompanied the collapse of British authority in 1947. It is difficult, therefore, to buy the self-serving imperial argument that Britain bequeathed to India its political unity and democracy.

I would argue, as Nehru did, that the idea of India has always been inherent in our civilization. This is why when Muhammad Ali Jinnah argued that religion was a valid determinant of nationhood and demanded a separate country for India's Muslims, Nehru never accepted his logic. To do so would have been to reduce India to a country of and for Hindus, and this, Nehru saw, would do violence to the idea of India that he cherished, valued so greatly and articulated so powerfully.

The Modern Nation-State

Earlier conceptions of India drew their inspiration from mythology and theology. However, the modern idea of India, despite the mystical influence of Tagore, and the spiritual and moral influences of Gandhiji, is a robustly secular and legal construct based upon the vision and intellect of our founding fathers, notably (in alphabetical order) Ambedkar, Nehru and Patel. The preamble of the Constitution itself is the most eloquent enumeration of this vision. In its description of the defining traits of the Indian republic, in its conception of justice, of liberty, of equality and fraternity, it firmly proclaims that the law will be the bedrock of the idea of India.

How did India preserve and protect a viable idea of itself in the course of the last seventy-two years, while it grew from 370 million people to 1.3 billion, reorganized its state structures, and sought to defend itself from internal and external dangers, all the while remaining democratic? I have tried to answer this question at length in my books. Certainly the accomplishment is extraordinary, and worthy of celebration. Amid India's myriad problems, it is democracy that has given Indians of every imaginable caste, creed, culture and cause the chance to break free of their age-old subsistence-level existence.

There is social oppression and caste tyranny, particularly in rural India, but Indian democracy offers the victims a means of escape, and often—thanks to the determination with which the poor and oppressed exercise their franchise—of triumph.

And yet, in the more than seven decades since Independence, democracy has failed to create a single political community. Instead, we have become more conscious than ever of what divides us: religion, region, caste, language, ethnicity. The political system has become looser and more fragmented. Politicians mobilize support along ever-narrower lines of political identity. It has become more important to be a 'backward caste', a 'tribal', or a religious sectarian than to be an Indian; and of course, to some it is more important to be a 'proud' Hindu than to be an Indian. This is particularly ironic because one of the early strengths of Nehruvian India—the survival of the nationalist movement as a political party, the Congress Party serving as an all-embracing, all-inclusive agglomeration of the major political tendencies in the country—stifled the normal process of contention over political principle. With the emergence and growth of other political forces, politicians have been tempted to organize themselves around identities other than party (or to create parties to reflect a specific identity).

Caste, which Nehru and his ilk abhorred and believed would disappear from the social matrix of modern India, has not merely survived and thrived, but has become an instrument for highly effective political mobilization. Candidates are picked by their parties with an eye towards the caste loyalties they can call upon; often their appeal is overtly to voters of their own caste or sub-caste, urging them to elect one of their own. The result has been the growth of caste-consciousness and casteism throughout society. In many states, caste determines educational opportunities, job prospects and governmental promotions; all too often, people say you cannot go forward unless you're a 'backward'.

Ironically, a distinctive feature of the Nehruvian legacy was its visionary rejection of India's assorted bigotries and particularism. All four generations of Nehrus in public life remained secular in outlook and conduct. Their appeal transcended caste, region, language and religion, something virtually impossible to say of most other leading Indian politicians.

Whether through elections or quotas, political mobilization in contemporary India has asserted the power of old identities, habits, faiths and prejudices. Transcending them will be a major challenge for the Indian polity in the twenty-first century.

One does question: what makes India a nation? In a country notorious for identity politics, especially at election time, we may well ask: what is an Indian's identity?

When an Italian nation was created in the second half of the nineteenth century out of a mosaic of principalities and small states, one Italian nationalist, Massimo Taparelli d'Azeglio, wrote: 'We have created Italy. Now all we need to do is to create Italians.'[10]

It is striking that, half a century later, no Indian nationalist succumbed to the temptation to express a similar thought. The prime exponent of modern Indian nationalism, Nehru, would never have spoken of 'creating Indians', because he believed that India and Indians had existed for millennia before he articulated their political aspirations in the twentieth century.

Nonetheless, the India that was born in 1947 was in a very real sense a new creation: a state that made fellow citizens of the Ladakhi and the Laccadivian, divided Punjabi from Punjabi and asked a Keralite peasant to feel allegiance to a Kashmiri Pandit ruling in Delhi, all for the first time.

Let me illustrate what this means with a simple story. When India celebrated the forty-ninth anniversary of its independence from British rule in 1996, our then prime minister, H.D. Deve Gowda, stood at the ramparts of Delhi's seventeenth-century Red

Fort and delivered the traditional Independence Day address to the nation in Hindi, one of India's official languages and its most widely spoken one. Ten other prime ministers had done exactly the same thing forty-eight times before him, but what was unusual this time was that Deve Gowda, a southerner from the state of Karnataka, spoke to the country in a language of which he did not know a word. Tradition and politics required a speech in Hindi, so he gave one—the words having been written out for him in his native Kannada script, in which they, of course, made no sense.

Such an episode is almost inconceivable elsewhere, but it represents the best of the oddities that help make India. Only in India could a country be ruled by a man who does not understand its 'national language'; only in India, for that matter, is there a 'national language' which half the population does not understand; and only in India could this particular solution be found to enable the prime minister to address his people. One of Indian cinema's finest 'playback singers', the Keralite K.J. Yesudas, sang his way to the top of the Hindi music charts with lyrics in that language written in the Malayalam script for him, but to see the same practice elevated to the prime ministerial address on Independence Day was a startling affirmation of Indian pluralism.

A Nation of Minorities

For, you see, we are all minorities in India. A typical Indian stepping off a train, a Hindi-speaking Hindu male from the Gangetic plains state of Uttar Pradesh (UP), might cherish the illusion that he represents the 'majority community', to use an expression much favoured by the less industrious of our journalists. But he does not. As a Hindu he belongs to the faith adhered to by some 81 per cent of the population, but the majority of the country does not speak Hindi; the majority does not hail from Uttar Pradesh; and if he were visiting, say, Kerala, he would discover that the majority there is not even male. Worse, our archetypal UP Hindu has only to mingle with the polyglot, multicoloured crowds (and I'm referring to the colour of their skins, not their clothes) thronging any of India's major railway stations to realize how much of a minority he really is. Even his Hinduism is no guarantee of majorityhood, because his caste automatically places him in a minority as well: if he is a Brahmin, 90 per cent of his fellow Indians are not; if he is a Yadav, a 'backward class', 85 per cent of Indians are not, and so on.

Or take language. The Constitution of India recognizes twenty-three today—our demonetized rupee notes give the denomination in fourteen languages—but in fact there are thirty-five Indian languages, which are spoken by more than a million people, and these are languages with their own scripts, grammatical structures and cultural assumptions, not just dialects (and if we were to count dialects within these languages, there are more than 22,000). Each of the native speakers of these languages is in a linguistic minority, for none enjoys majority status in India. Thanks in part to the popularity of Bombay's Hindi cinema, Hindi is understood, if not always well spoken, by nearly half the population of India, but it is in no sense the language of the majority; indeed, its locutions, gender rules and script are unfamiliar to most Indians in the south or north-east.

Ethnicity further complicates the notion of a majority community. Most of the time, an Indian's name immediately reveals where he is from and what his mother tongue is; when we introduce ourselves we are advertising our origins. Despite some intermarriage at the elite levels in cities, Indians still largely remain endogamous, and a Bengali is easily distinguished from a Punjabi. The difference this reflects is often more apparent than the elements of commonality. A Karnataka Brahmin shares his Hindu faith with a Bihari Kurmi, but feels little identity with him in respect of appearance, dress, customs, tastes, language or political objectives. At the same time a Tamil Hindu would feel that he has far more in common with a Tamil Christian or Muslim than with, say, a Haryanvi Jat with whom he formally shares religion.

Why do I harp on these differences? Only to make the point that Indian nationalism is a rare animal indeed. This land imposes no narrow conformities on its citizens: you can be many things and one thing. You can be a good Muslim, a good Keralite and a good Indian all at once. When Yugoslavia was tearing itself apart in a civil war among peoples all descended from the same Slavic tribes that had settled in the Balkan peninsula a millennium earlier, learned Freudians pointed to the disagreements that arise out of 'the narcissism of minor differences'. But in India we celebrate the commonality of major differences. To stand Michael Ignatieff's famous phrase on its head, we are a land of belonging rather than of blood.

So Indian nationalism is not based on any of the conventional indices of national identity. Not language, not ethnicity, since 'Indian' accommodates a diversity of racial types in which many Indians (Punjabis and Bengalis, in particular) have more ethnically in common with foreigners (Pakistanis and Bangladeshis) than with their other compatriots (Poonawallas and Bangaloreans).

Not religion, since India is a secular pluralist state that is home to every religion known to mankind, with the possible exception of Shintoism.

Not geography, since the natural geography of the subcontinent—framed by the mountains and the sea—was hacked by Partition in 1947.

And not even territory, since, by law, anyone with one grandparent born in pre-Partition India—outside the territorial boundaries of today's state—is eligible for citizenship. Indian nationalism has therefore always been the nationalism of an idea.

It is the idea of an ever-ever land—emerging from an ancient civilization, united by a shared history, sustained by pluralist democracy. India's democracy imposes no narrow conformities on its citizens.

So the idea of India is one land embracing many. Geography helps, because it accustoms Indians to the idea of difference.

A Profusion of Religions

The Indian idea, as I have long argued, is that a nation may endure differences of caste, creed, colour, conviction, culture, cuisine, costume and custom, and still rally around a consensus. And that consensus is around the simple idea that in a democracy you don't really need to agree—except on the ground rules of how you will disagree.

My generation grew up in an India where our sense of nationhood lay in the slogan 'unity in diversity'. We were brought up to take pluralism for granted, and to reject the communalism that had partitioned the nation when the British left. In rejecting the case for Pakistan, Indian nationalism also rejected the very idea that religion should be a determinant of nationhood. We never fell into the insidious trap of agreeing that, since Partition had established a state for Muslims, what remained was a state for Hindus. To accept the idea of India you had to spurn the logic that had divided the country.

This was what that much-abused term 'secularism' meant for us. Western dictionaries defined secularism as the absence of religion, but Indian secularism meant a profusion of religions; the state engaged with all of them but privileged none. Secularism in India did not mean irreligiousness, which even avowedly atheist parties such as the communists or the southern Dravida Munnetra Kazhagam (DMK) party found unpopular amongst their voters; indeed, in Kolkata's annual Durga Puja, the communist parties compete with each other to put up the most lavish puja pandals, pavilions to the goddess Durga. Rather, secularism meant, in the Indian tradition, multireligiousness. The Kolkata neighbourhood I described earlier epitomized this India.

Throughout the decades after Independence, the political culture of the country reflected these secular assumptions and attitudes. Though the Indian population is nearly 80 per cent Hindu and the country had been partitioned as a result of a demand for a separate Muslim homeland, three of India's fourteen presidents have been Muslims; so were innumerable governors, cabinet ministers, chief ministers of states, ambassadors, generals and Supreme Court justices (and chief justices). During the war with Pakistan in 1971, the Indian Air Force in the northern sector was commanded by a Muslim (Idris Hasan Latif); the army commander was a Parsi (Sam Manekshaw); the general officer commanding-in-chief of the forces that marched into Bangladesh was a Sikh (Jagjit Singh Aurora), and the general flown in to negotiate the surrender of the Pakistani forces in East Bengal was Jewish (J.F.R. Jacob). *That* is India.

Not all agree with this vision of India. There are those who wish it to become a Hindu Rashtra, a land of and for the Hindu majority; they have made gains in the elections of this decade and in the politics of the street. Secularism is established in India's Constitution, but they ask why India should not, like many other Third World countries, find refuge in the assertion of what they call its own religious identity. We have all seen the outcome of this view in the horrors that have cost perhaps 2000 lives in Gujarat more than a decade and a half ago.

Those riots, like the killing of Sikhs in reaction to Indira Gandhi's assassination in 1984, were fundamentally violative of the idea of India. India has survived the Aryans, the Mughals, the British; it has taken from each—language, art, food, learning—and grown with all of them. To be Indian is to be a part of an elusive dream we all share, a dream that fills our minds with sounds, words, flavours from many sources that we cannot easily identify. Large, eclectic, agglomerative, the Hinduism that I know understands that faith is a matter of hearts and minds, not of bricks and stone. 'Build Rama in your heart', the Hindu is enjoined, and if Rama is in your heart, it will matter little where else he is, or is not.

Chauvinism and anti-minority violence have emerged from the competition for resources in a contentious democracy. Politicians of all faiths across India seek to mobilize voters by appealing to narrow identities; by seeking votes in the name of religion, caste and region, they have urged voters to define themselves on these lines. As religion, caste and region have come to dominate public discourse, to some it has become more important to be a Muslim, a Bodo or a Yadav than to be an Indian.

This is why the change in the public discourse about Indianness is so dangerous. The notion of majority and minority, as I have suggested, is fundamentally un-Indian and fails to reflect the real nature of our society. The suggestion that only a Hindu, and only a certain kind of Hindu, can be an authentic Indian is an affront to the very premise of Indian nationalism. An India that denies itself to some of us could end up being denied to all of us.

As the past is used by some to haunt the present, the cycle of violence goes on, spawning new hostages to history, ensuring that future generations will be taught new wrongs to set right. We live, Octavio Paz once wrote, between oblivion and memory. Memory and oblivion: how one leads to the other, and back again, has been the concern of much of my fiction. As I pointed out in the last words of my novel *Riot*,[11] history is not a web woven with innocent hands.

The reduction of any group of Indians to second-class status in their homeland is unthinkable. It would be a second Partition, and a partition in the Indian soul would be as bad as a partition in the Indian soil.

My idea of India celebrates diversity: if the USA is a melting pot, as I have long argued, then to me India is a thali, a selection of sumptuous dishes in different bowls. Each tastes different, and does not necessarily mix with the next, but they belong together on the same plate, and they complement each other in making the meal a satisfying repast.

This is the idea of India that we must defend at all costs. India's founding fathers wrote a Constitution for their dreams; we have given passports to their ideals. Today these ideals are contested not only by stone-throwing young men in the streets of Srinagar and rifle-wielding Maoists in the forests of Chhattisgarh, but also by self-righteous triumphalists in the ruling party who proclaim that all Indians must subscribe to their narrow vision of Hindutva as an alternative to a more capacious Indianness.

They advocate a nationalism that is divisive rather than inclusive, embodied in a chauvinism intolerant of diversity and difference.

My idea of India gives me the right to chant 'Bharat Mata ki Jai'. It also gives me the right not to say it if I don't wish to. This is the right the custodians of today's nationalism would take away from me.

This is a battle for India's soul. All of us who believe in the liberal values embodied in our Constitution must strive to ensure that the ultimate winner must be the idea of India. Indians must remain faithful to our founding values of the twentieth century if we are to conquer the twenty-first.

Secularism: Central to a Democratic Nation

Neera Chandhoke

For I have neither wit, nor words, nor worth,
Action, nor utterance, nor the power of speech,
To stir men's blood. I only speak right on.
l tell you that which you yourselves do know.[1]

Affirming Secularism and Democracy

The results of the 2019 general elections in India confirmed the lurking fear that has hovered like a dark cloud over our political horizon since 2014. India is a multireligious country, but we now see the consolidation of the Hindu vote across caste and across class. This consolidation has brought the religious right back into power with an improved majority. Election rhetoric had ridiculed political leaders who stood from minority-dominated constituencies; appealed to a narrow, religion-based nationalism; evoked fear that Pakistan threatened the body politic; and raised aloft the banner of national security over other concerns. None of the planks that garnered rich dividends had anything to do with what are often called 'real facts', but fiery rhetoric won over mundane issues of a declining economy and increasing unemployment. A victorious prime minister told his national constituency: 'Secularism was a tax that used to be paid till today. Fake secularism and its leaders who were calling for the secular forces to unite have been exposed.'[2] Exposed, one may ask, as what? As Indians committed to the dignity of all and discrimination against none? Or as citizens who want passionately to defend the plural character of Indian society?

The prime minister is not politically naive; he surely knows that political commitments that run against ruling ideologies do not fade into the twilight with the coming into power of a new government. These commitments might not be palatable to the new ruling class, but they continue to inhabit democratic imaginations, continue to act as signposts to a road that leads to a good life for all, and continue to act as a watchdog of ruling dispensations. Criticism of the government and its policies lies at the heart of democratic society, at the heart of the political project to hold elected power elites accountable for their acts of omission and commission.

In any case, democracy is not reducible to election results. Elections are one—albeit significant and decisive—moment of democracy. Democracy establishes and maintains a conversation between the citizens and their representatives. Elections decide who these representatives will be. The process of holding these representatives accountable does not cease with the results of an election. It holds good, no matter who holds power, or with what majority. For that reason, it is democracy, not just elections, of which we should speak, and it is the democratic spirit which we should, and will, uphold.

Secularism, let me hasten to add, is a companion concept of democracy. It is an extension of Article 14 of the Constitution— the right to equality, to all religious groups in the public domain. Secularism is not a stand-alone concept; it is an integral part of the democratic imaginary, a principle that holds that no one should be discriminated against for reasons that are purely arbitrary, such as birth into a specific community. It follows that secularism is distinct from secularization, which is a social concept that captures the phenomenon of privatization of religion in Europe during the Enlightenment. Secularism is a political principle that supports democracy, and is justified by democracy. Secularization of society was once thought of as an essential precondition for secularism. This belief has retreated in the face of politicized religion in the public sphere in many countries of Europe. Finally, secularism is not, as is popularly understood, the binary opposite of religion or communalism. Secularism is opposed to theocracy, or to the fusion of religious and political power. The fusion of two categories of awesome power is hardly democratic, quite the contrary.

In a democracy, the Constitution separates forms of power, and all forms of power are subject to limits placed by the Constitution. Secularism is a companion concept of democracy but is not reducible to democracy. This gains some relevance when we recollect that we are not speaking of religion as faith. People can be religious in their private lives. They do not need to harness their faith to a political project of capture of power. What secularism combats is politicized power, power harnessed to a religious anchor, religious identities as power. It is precisely this development that our leaders tried to counter during the freedom struggle. Secularism was an attempt to control politicized religion from taking over the state. This was absolutely indispensable because the country had been partitioned on the basis of religion. The reasons why secularism was adopted in this form, and not as classically understood as the separation of religion and the non-religious, has to do with our history.

The Evolution of Secularism

For centuries, Hindus and Muslims had lived together, even if on balance they did not live together very well. Taboos on diet and on inter-social relations had long marked social relationships. Yet both communities shared a language, common memories, rituals, music, and worshipped together at the shrines of Muslim saints. People may or may not be inclined towards religiosity, and yet they might hesitate to dine and socialize with, let alone marry, members of another community. But this does not mean that they ritually inflict harm on them. We can believe that others have their own reasons for thinking and doing what they think and do, and we have different reasons for thinking and doing what we wish to do. These are some of the modalities by which groups in society identify themselves and distinguish themselves from others. For these reasons, they construct symbolic and often spatial barriers between themselves and others.

At precisely this point of the argument we must pause. The bracketing-off of identities is a sociological phenomenon. Despite these social barriers, forms of cooperation can and do arise in the workplace, in social and political organizations, in and through movements, and through associational life. Social relations between Hindus and Muslims were shaped by prohibitions on many counts. But we also read of notable exceptions to the generic principle. All communities, as suggested above, shared much in common, from worship at roadside shrines, to the languages of everyday existence, to common historical memories, to the habits of quotidian life.

Notably, when these bracketed identities are transformed as weapons to be deployed for symbolic or material gain, a sociological phenomenon translates into a political movement that lays claims upon the body politic. The politicization of identities invariably leads to open and ruthless competition for all sorts of power, often at the cost of human lives. We must also recognize that the translation of often hidden animosities into violence involves a trigger. This trigger is usually provided by organizations that belong to cadres of the religious right that are found in all religious communities and/ or entrepreneurs and merchants of hate who excel in excavating what might be hidden sentiments of resentment against other communities and in playing up incidents that otherwise can be passed off as minor. These entrepreneurs do not belong to any specific community, they have no loyalty, and are most often than not mercenaries up for sale to the highest bidder.

The tragedy is that the trigger stokes and evokes hellfires of hatred, devastating violence and eternal damnation. In India, the consolidation of communal organizations triggered off the brutalization of social and political identities, creation of divides, exacerbation of hitherto muted schisms and the creation of new ones. Some very toxic processes resulted in brutal communal riots between Hindus and Muslims from the late years of the nineteenth century, right up to the last years of British imperialism, 1946–47.

The backdrop of Partition was designed, implemented, hammered down and nailed to the mast of politicized religious identities. By the first two decades of the twentieth century, India witnessed the eruption of competitive nationalism harnessed to the nation–state project. This was legitimized by the two-nation theory, and the demand for a separate state. The nation-making project and competitive nationalism that hinged on a demand for a 'state of one's own' culminated in the multiple tragedies that followed the partition of India. This was also the time that India became independent of colonial rule and a new country called Pakistan was created out of northern and eastern India.

This is the irony of our independence. When we read about the coming of independence to India in 1947, we read stories of how thousands and millions of people came together in a spectacular anti-imperialist struggle, of harsh punishments meted out to freedom fighters, of imprisonments, of mass killings as in Jallianwala Bagh, of non-cooperation movements and lathi charges, of memorable books written within prison walls about the past and the future of India by Jawaharlal Nehru, of solidarity, and of sacrifice. We read of a man called Mohandas Karamchand Gandhi who was ready to inflict suffering on himself rather than allow suffering to be inflicted on the souls and bodies of others. But we are also told stories of the great religious divide between Hindus and Muslims, which flared up into collective violence episodically, and of the partition that occurred at exactly the same time as Independence. In effect the Independence of India was contingent upon Partition. The sort of communal violence that rent the air was sufficient cause for concern, for thinking about the sort of polity that India should be.

The Road to Secularism

Communal violence was not invented in 1947. Riots since the beginning of the twentieth century inexorably led to the partition of India. There was no other option given the charged times. But it is not as if the leaders did not try to pre-empt Partition. In 1931, a savage riot in Kanpur left hundreds dead. Parts of the city were destroyed, mosques and temples were damaged, and houses burnt. A miasma of devastation and gloom hung over the city. In the aftermath of the Kanpur riots, the Indian National Congress established an enquiry commission to explore the reasons for the violence. A small committee of prominent Congressmen, Purushottam Das Tandon, Abdul Majeed Khwaja, T.A.K. Sherwani, Zafarul Mulk, Pandit Sunderlal and Bhagwan Das, authored a report[3] that was an extended and comprehensive statement of the analysis of communalism and the objectives of the freedom struggle.

Communal riots are an outcome, the authors of the report suggested persuasively, of certain historical and social processes sparked off by colonial rule. The argument overturned the assumption, widely disseminated by the colonial government, that Hindu–Muslim enmity had existed in the past, continues into the present, and is bound to project itself in the future. The maintenance of peace required the presence of British rule. No other agent could provide India with the stability which could stave off continuous and inevitable communal riots. This was held to be the justification of imperial rule.

The Indian National Congress accepted the term 'communal', which was widely believed to be an invention of colonialism, but held that it was the British policy of divide and rule that was responsible for the violence, loss of lives, and massive destruction that were the direct outcomes of the communal riots. The official position of the Congress was that India was home to both Hindus and Muslims, and that it was possible to put an end to the conflict through the use of political imaginations, empathy and consideration for minority communities. Minorities had to be sure that their rights to religion and culture would be given full protection in an independent India.

In the shadow of the Kanpur riot, the Congress drafted the Karachi Resolution on Fundamental Rights. The Resolution emphasized the right to religion and the freedom to profess and practise any religion. The minorities had the right to cultural autonomy, and equal access to educational facilities. On 31 March 1931, Gandhi, moving the Resolution on Fundamental Rights in the open session of the Congress at Karachi, spoke on the issue. Though Islamic and Aryan cultures are not mutually exclusive, he said, we must recognize that Mussalmans look upon Islamic culture as distinctive from Aryan. Let us therefore cultivate tolerance.[4] Religious neutrality is another important provision, he continued. Swaraj will favour Hinduism no more than Islam, nor Islam more than Hinduism. Let us from now on, he concluded, adopt the principle of state neutrality in our daily affairs. The three principles that were to govern democratic India henceforth were secularism, minority rights and tolerance.

The report of the Sapru Committee,[5] set up by the non-party conference in November 1944, recommended full religious tolerance, non-interference in religious beliefs, practices and institutions, and protection of the language and culture of minority communities. The report proposed that in every state, and at the centre, a commission consisting of a representative of each minority community would be set up to keep a watch on the affairs of the minorities.

Arguably, three features distinguished the official position of the Congress on communal violence. One, the leaders accepted that the Hindu majority was as guilty of communal sentiments and violence as the Muslim minority. Two, because Indian society was religious, and because religion had been given a public face as politics and as ideology, the state had to be secular or neutral towards religions. A democratic state had no other option. Three, group rights for minorities were not only an essential precondition for individual rights, but important in themselves. In other words, religion was seen as a significant good to which all people had a right. In a society where the Hindu community had the advantage of numbers, minorities had to be protected against the onslaught of majoritarianism. A malevolent fate, however, decreed otherwise.

Despite earnest assurances, the trail of repeated communal riots in the twenty-seven years before Independence had traumatized the body politic. The leaders of the freedom movement were faced with a terrible choice. Independence could only come at the cost of the partition of India and her people. This had become historically inevitable. Moreover, religion as politics and politicized religion could not be brushed off as a minor or even major inconvenience, transitory and fugitive. It was futile to hope that religion would be privatized at some time in the future, and the public sphere would be free of the constant threat of communal violence. It was precisely this violence that prompted one of India's tallest leaders, Jawaharlal Nehru, to write in his diary while in prison in 1935, 'What a disgustingly savage people we are . . . politics, progress, socialism, communism, science—where are they before this black religious savagery?' His biographer S. Gopal concluded that Nehru was extremely impatient with religion. It might be an anchor for some, but he did not seek harbourage in this way. 'I prefer the open sea,' wrote Nehru, 'with all its storms and tempests.'[6]

Nehru had to change his position when the Partition riots took place. He had to accept regretfully that not only were Indians religious, religion had been politicized to an alarming degree and latched on to the dangerous dreams of a nation and a state of one's own. As the country entered the mid-decade of the 1940s, it was clear that independence from British rule loomed on the horizon. At the same time, the prospect of independence was compromised by the division of hearts and minds, hearths and workplaces, shared histories, languages, cultures, music, literature and rituals. The two moments came together in August 1947.

One would have expected Nehru, a secularist in the Western mode, to banish religion from the public sphere of politics as Kemal Atatürk had done in Turkey, and force the notion of religion as private faith upon his people. But that would have been bad history as well as bad politics. Religion in India was not simply faith. An entire brand of politics that ranged from awareness of religious identity and consequent politicization to competitive nationalism and to Partition had been constructed around religion. Since both the pervasiveness as well as the political potency of religion had caught hold of the public mind, Nehru could hardly ignore the command of religious politics in the public sphere. Nor could he abdicate his responsibility, that of calming down religious passions. What he could do was to oversee that the future of India was civilized, civil, secure, democratic and secular.

India after Independence

Though Congress leaders used the term 'secularism' in the pre-Independence period often, oddly enough the concept was never spelt out or elaborated as a principle of state policy. Nor did it form part of the preamble to the Constitution until 1976, vide the forty-second amendment. But the seeds of secularism were present throughout the debates in the Constituent Assembly. For instance, most members agreed that the preamble to the Constitution should not contain any reference to God. On 17 October 1949, during discussions on the wording of the preamble, H.V. Kamath moved an amendment that the preamble should begin with the phrase 'In the name of God'. Similar amendments were moved by Shibban Lal Saxena and Pandit Mohan Malaviya. Other members objected, and a majority of the members expressed their conviction that religion was a matter of individual choice and not the signpost of a collective.[7]

Pandit H.N. Kunzru stated with regret that a matter concerning our innermost and sacred feelings had been brought into the arena of discussion. It would be far more consistent with our beliefs that we should not impose our feelings on others, and that the collective view should not be forced on others. 'We invoke the name of God, but I make bold to say that while we do so, we are showing a narrow sectarian spirit, which is contrary to the spirit of the Constitution.'[8] The amendment moved by Kamath was defeated.

It is quite puzzling that though copious references were made to secularism, no one seemed to be quite sure what the concept stood for. It was on 24 January 1948 that Prime Minister Jawaharlal Nehru clarified the notion of secularism in a convocation address at Aligarh Muslim University. In the middle of a fluid state caused by Partition, he said, all of us have to be clear about our basic allegiance to certain ideas. Do we, he asked, believe in a national state, which includes people of all religions and shades of opinion and is essentially secular as a state, or do we believe in the religious, theocratic conception of a state that considers people of other faiths as beyond the pale? The idea of a theocratic state was given up some time ago by the world and it has no place in the mind of a modern person. And yet the question has to be put in India, for some of us have tried to jump to a bygone age. Whatever confusion, he said, the present may contain, in the future, India will be a land, as in the past, of many faiths equally honoured and respected, within a tolerant, creative nationalism, not a narrow nationalism living in its own shell.[9]

In 1961, in a preface to a work on secularism, *Dharam Nirpeksh Raj* by Raghunath Singh, Prime Minister Nehru further elaborated the concept of secularism. We, he said, call our state a secular state. There is no good Hindi word for secular. Some people think it means opposed to religion. But this, he wrote, is not the correct notion of secularism. It means a state that honours all faiths equally and gives them equal opportunities, that as a state it does not allow itself to be attached to one faith or religion, which then becomes the state religion. This is a modern conception. In India, we have a long history of toleration, but this not all that secularism is about.[10]

Strictly speaking we do not need to proclaim secularism in order to grant religious freedom. This freedom can emerge from, and form part of, Article 19 guaranteeing the fundamental right to liberty that is assured to every citizen. But a secular state cannot stop at granting the right to religious freedom. The principle of secularism goes further and establishes *equality* between all religious groups. But then the generic right to equality granted by Article 14 of the Fundamental Rights Chapter can protect equality among religious communities. If we were to stop at this, secularism would be rendered unnecessary, it could well be collapsed into democracy. Secularism extends beyond equality and freedom in two ways. As a companion concept of democracy, secularism extends individual rights to equality to religious communities and guarantees equality among them. Two, the state is not aligned to any religion. These *commitments establish the credentials of a secular state.* Or secularism, we can say, promises that the state would neither align itself with any one religion—especially the majority religion—nor pursue any religious tasks of its own, and ensures that religious minorities are treated equally by the state.

The second and the third component of secularism—equality of all religions, and the distancing of the state from all religious groups—was specifically meant to assure the minorities that they had a legitimate place as citizens in the country, and that they would not be discriminated against. Correspondingly, secularism established that the majority group would not be privileged in any manner. The creed simply discouraged any pretension that a demographically numerous religious group had any right to stamp the body politic with its ethos.

In the Supreme Court

Given that secularism had not been defined in the Constitution and did not form part of the preamble until the 1970s, given that the meaning Nehru allotted to the concept was not codified in law, and above all given that the concept is neither self-evident nor self-explanatory, the task of defining and elaborating the concept of secularism has fallen upon the shoulders of the Supreme Court. On 27 October 2016, amidst an acrimonious legal debate on curbing the role of religion in electioneering, the Supreme Court rhetorically asked whether secularism meant the complete separation of religion from politics. The bench concluded that secularism does not mean that the state should stay aloof from religion, but that it should give equal treatment to every religion. Religion and caste are vital aspects of our polity and it is not possible to completely separate them from politics.[11]

The Supreme Court reiterated an earlier ruling in the case of *S.R. Bommai vs the Union of India* in 1993. The set of judgments in the Bommai case are lengthy and complex but we can isolate the following themes that are of interest to the argument at hand.[12] One, secularism is part of the basic structure of the Constitution and therefore cannot be amended. Two, secularism is derived from the cultural *principle* of tolerance and ensures the equality of religions. The cultural principle is referred to as 'sarva dharma sama bhava'. Three, the Court reiterated Nehru's opinion that no religion will be at risk in a secular India, because the government will not be aligned to religion. Four, Justice Ramaswamy ruled that there is an essential connection between secularism and democracy; the concept of the secular state is needed for the working of democracy, and the realization of social and economic needs that are essential for material and moral prosperity and political justice. In effect, the highest court of the land extended recognition to and legitimized a public doctrine based on neo-Vedanta which had become one of the creeds of the freedom struggle. This was defined as secularism.

There is perhaps a need to secularize secularism for a multireligious society.

Democracy and Secularism

How can we recover secularism in and for a plural society that is wracked with anxieties about its own pretensions to democracy, and about the many injustices that have led to violence and disregard for the human condition? Let us take stock of secularism within the context of democracy, and see what perhaps a reworked concept of secularism would look like. If the basic aim of secularism as it has historically developed in India is to secure equality of all religious denominations, *the concept of secularism is* derived from the principle of equality. In fact, let me suggest that secularism gains meaning and substance only when we see it as legitimate from the perspective of democracy and its core principle of equality. Logically, there is no reason why a society should be committed to secularism, unless it is committed beforehand to the concept of equality.

Secularism can, justifiably, be interpreted as a companion concept of democracy. Both democracy and secularism are constitutive of a just state, a state that ensures equality of status between individuals, as well as between religious communities. Democracy takes care of the first avatar of justice, the equal right of all individuals to certain goods. Secularism secures the second avatar of justice, that religious groups are not disadvantaged for arbitrary and irrelevant reasons, and that these groups have equal moral standing in society.

Six points might be in order before concluding the argument. One, secularism per se has little to do with inequality or injustice within religious groups. These fall within the province of democracy. Secularism is concerned about a weak form of equality, or non-discrimination between religious groups. The norm ensures that the state should not be aligned to one group that for this reason acquires dominance. Two, secularism is part of the democratic imaginary and is not a stand-alone concept. Three, secularism is not a robust concept like democracy or justice, it is a 'thin' and limited procedural concept. Four, though secularism has been presented as the binary opposite of religion, or in India, communalism, it is the binary opposite of theocratic states bringing together religious and political power in one set of hands, mainly the civilian executive, or the army. Five, the challenge to secularism has not come from personal faith or religion, but from religious groups that struggle for power or against power and domination. Six, the challenge is to democracy because denial of secularism catapults issues about the rights and privileges of citizenship and throws into sharp relief the intersections between religion and other concerns such as lack of voice, inadequate distribution of goods, and recognition of the distinctiveness of groups.

The play on the term is neither informative, illuminating, nor particularly interesting. It speaks of narrow and prejudiced minds, of limited horizons and lack of imaginations. It tells us of people who cannot tolerate other communities as fellow citizens because they are caught up in claustrophobic worlds of their own.

More seriously, secularism is today caught in a maelstrom of frustrated expectations and hopes belied. It is in crisis, not because it is irrelevant, but because it has been subjected to rank overuse and invested with far too many expectations in the past. The concept has been summoned to perform various and arguably too many functions in our postcolonial society, from national integration to gender justice. In the vocabulary of many an undemocratic political leader, it even stands in for democracy. Unable to bear the weight of too many political projects and ambitions, the overburdened concept of secularism shows signs of imploding.

In history, secularism rode to prominence on the back of secularization. Now that secularization or the privatization of religion has been shown up as one of the vanities of modernity, secularism needs a new home. What other home can our world provide secularism except democracy. These are not good times to defend secularism, it is true, but soldier on we must. Therefore, let us act as the conscience of the nation, and take heart from Jawaharlal Nehru's words in *The Discovery of India*. He quotes the chorus from *The Bacchae of Euripides*, translated by Gilbert Murray: 'What else is Wisdom? What of man's endeavour/Or God's high grace, so lovely and so great? To stand from fear set free, to breathe and wait/To hold a hand uplifted over Hate, and shall not Loveliness be loved for ever?'[13]

We have to conquer hate through secularism and democracy.

Indian Nationalism versus Hindutva Nationalism

Sitaram Yechury

The results of the 2019 general elections in India marked the consolidation of the political right. The sweep of the victory and the manner in which it was achieved define the impending challenges for both our people and our secular democratic Republic.

The RSS–BJP combine successfully shifted the poll narrative away from the day-to-day livelihood concerns of the people. The last couple of years saw the peoples' discontent expressed in various protest actions and movements. However, the terrorist attack in Pulwama on 14 February 2019 followed by the subsequent Air Force bombing in Balakot (Pakistan) on 26 February were successfully utilized to mount a new narrative. The RSS–BJP combine was able to successfully run a campaign centred around nationalist jingoism. The sharpening of communal polarization that took place over the last five years dovetailed with this, creating a communal, nationalist, jingoistic narrative. The larger-than-life projection of the Modi persona provided the principal actor for the unfolding of this narrative. Largely, the 2019 elections were more in the nature of presidential rather than parliamentary elections. Eventually, the candidates did not matter and the voting took place on the basis of emotions generated by this narrative for a Modi government. This narrative fit neatly into the RSS construct of the elections as a battle against terrorism emanating from 'Muslim Pakistan' targeting 'Hindu India'.[1]

The success achieved by the RSS–BJP could not have been possible but for the humongous money power displayed in these elections.[2] Corporate media was enlisted through corporate donations of unprecedented magnitude to unleash a propaganda offensive that went unmatched.[3] Independent constitutional authorities such as the Election Commission also played a role in permitting such a propaganda blitzkrieg, violating all norms and political moral codes.[4]

A corporate communal alliance has come into dominance, vigorously propagating the ideology of aggrandizing nationalism, putting the 'nation' and its interests above the people, demanding sacrifices from the people including the forfeiture of their democratic rights in the name of the 'nation'. The leaders of the current government in India often proclaim that 'freedom of expression cannot be at the expense of the nation'![5] Recently, when the amendments to the National Investigation Agency (NIA) Act were being considered by the Lok Sabha, the home minister thundered that those who opposed the amendments were supporting terrorism and protecting terrorists, statements that can be inferred even from the official report of the government.[6] These draconian amendments severely impinge on the democratic rights and civil liberties of all individuals. Any expression of dissent against the BJP government and its policies can lead to arrest and detention, on the grounds of being 'anti-national'—the legalization of a 'police state'.

The challenge to this right-wing political consolidation will necessarily have to come from the left and left-of-centre political consolidation. This can, however, succeed only when there is clarity over what is at stake.

What is at stake is the very survival of our secular, democratic, constitutional order. It is the very survival of modern India as contained in the expression 'idea of India'.

'Idea of India': Backdrop and Evolution

The emergence of nation states was integral to the long process of transition of human civilization from feudalism to capitalism. This period also threw up in Europe the struggle for the separation of the state from the church. The triumph of capitalism over feudalism, at the same time, signified the separation of the political authority from the myth of a divine sanction to rule invoked by kings and emperors across several civilizations at the peak of feudalism.

The agreements of Westphalia, finally signed in 1648, laid the principles of sovereignty of the nation state and the consequent international laws, and are widely believed to have established an international system on the basis of the principle of sovereignty of states, equality between states, and non-intervention of one state in the internal affairs of another state, usually referred to as the Westphalian system. Westphalian peace was negotiated in the period 1644–48 between major European powers. These treaties laid the basis for a host of international laws, many of which remain in force today.

During the course of the defeat of fascism in the Second World War and the consequent dynamics of decolonization, the people's struggles for freedom from colonial rule threw up many constructs regarding the character of these independent countries. For sure, such constructs arose out of a long struggle in individual countries against colonialism, including India, during this period.

The concept of the 'idea of India' emerged during the epic people's struggle for India's freedom from British colonialism. What is this 'idea of India'? To put it in simple terms, though conscious of its complexity and multiple dimensions, this concept represents the idea that India as a country moves towards transcending its immense diversities in favour of a substantially inclusive unity of its people.

In his introduction to a *Seminar* special issue containing revised versions of lectures on the relations between politics and political economy in India given at a 2010 seminar at the Heyman Center for the Humanities at Columbia University, New York, Akeel Bilgrami says the following about my observations on the 'idea of India':

> [This] might be viewed as an ideal of a nation that rejects the entire trajectory in Europe that emerged after the Westphalian peace. What emerged then (and there) was a compulsion to seek legitimacy for a new kind of state, one that could no longer appeal to older notions of the 'divine right' of states personified in their monarchs. It sought this legitimacy in a new form of political psychology of a new kind of subject, the 'citizen', a psychology based on a *feeling* for a new form of entity that had emerged, the 'nation'. This feeling, which came to be called 'nationalism', had to be generated in the populace of citizens, and the standard process that was adopted in Europe for generating it was to find an *external* enemy *within*, the outsider, the 'other' in one's midst (the Irish, the Jews, to name just two) to be despised and subjugated. In a somewhat later time, with the addition of a more numerical and statistical form of discourse, these came to be called 'minorities' and the method by which this feeling for the nation was created came to be called 'majoritarianism'.[7]

The RSS–BJP objective of replacing the secular democratic modern Indian Republic with their concept of a 'Hindu Rashtra' is, in a sense, a 'throwback' to the Westphalian nation-state model where national majorities control the state, and hence minorities are at their mercy. In this case, the Hindu majority subjugates other religious minorities (mainly Muslim: the *external* enemy *within*) to foster 'Hindu nationalism' as against 'Indian nationhood'.[8] Ironically, it is they who import the Western concept of a nation and impose it over Indian experience. This, in fact, represents a *throwback* to notions of nationalism that dominated the intellectual discourse prior to the sweep of the Indian people's struggle for freedom. Such a state, based on 'majoritarianism'—their version of a rabidly intolerant fascistic 'Hindu Rashtra'—negates the core around which emerged the consciousness of Indian nationhood contained in the 'idea of India' as a reflection of the emergence of 'a political psychology of a new kind'.[9]

RSS–BJP ideologues dismiss the 'idea of India' as a mere idea—a metaphysical concept. They reassert as a given reality Indian (Hindu) nationalism, negating the epic freedom struggle of the Indian people. From this struggle emerged the concept of Indian nationhood, rising above the Westphalian concept. By contrast, Bilgrami claims: 'The prodigious and sustained mobilization of its masses that India witnessed over the last three crucial decades of the freedom struggle could not have been possible without an alternative and *inclusionary* ideal of this kind to inspire it.'[10]

India's diversity—linguistic, religious, ethnic, cultural, etc.—is incomparably vaster than any other country that the world knows of. Officially, it has been recorded that there are at least 1618 languages in India; 6400 castes; six major religions, four of which originated in these lands; and six anthropologically defined ethnic groups. All this put together is being politically administered as one country. A measure of this diversity is that India celebrates twenty-nine major religio-cultural festivals and probably has the largest number of religious holidays amongst all the countries of the world.

Those who argue that it was the British who united this vast diversity ignore the fact that it was the British who engineered the partition of the subcontinent leading to over a million deaths and a communal transmigration of a colossal order. British colonialism has the ignominious history of leaving behind legacies that continue to fester as wounds through the partition of countries they had colonized—Palestine, Cyprus, countries in Africa, apart from the Indian subcontinent. It is the pan-Indian people's struggle for freedom that united this diversity and integrated more than 660 feudal princely states into modern India, giving shape to a pan-Indian consciousness.

Battle of Visions

The emergence of the conception of the 'idea of India' was a product of the Indian people's freedom struggle. It arose from a continuous battle between three visions that emerged during the course of India's struggle for freedom in the 1920s over the content of the character of independent India. The mainstream Congress vision had articulated that independent India should be a secular democratic Republic. The left, while agreeing with this objective, went further to envision that the political freedom of the country must be extended to achieve the socio-economic freedom of every individual, possible only under socialism.

Antagonistic to both these was a third vision which argued that the character of independent India should be determined by the religious affiliations of its people. This vision had a twin expression— the Muslim League championing a 'Muslim nation state' and the RSS championing a 'Hindu Rashtra'. The former succeeded with the unfortunate partition of the country, engineered, aided and abetted by the British colonial rulers, with all its consequences that continue to fester tensions to date.

The latter, having failed to achieve their objective at the time of independence, continued with their efforts to transform modern India into their project of a rabidly intolerant, fascistic 'Hindu Rashtra'. Mahatma Gandhi's assassination reflected the disappointment over the fact that the Indian freedom movement rejected the RSS vision and political project.

Clearly, the ideological battles and political conflicts in contemporary India are a continuation of the battle between these three visions. Needless to add, the contours of this battle will define the direction and content of the process of the realization of the 'idea of India'.

Role of the Left

The Indian left played an important role in this process of the evolution of this 'idea of India'. Indeed, for this very reason, given the left's visionary commitments to the long struggle for freedom, the left's role is absolutely central to the realization of the 'idea of India' in today's conditions.

Let me illustrate this with reference to three issues that continue to constitute the core of the 'idea of India'. The struggles on the land question unleashed by the communists in various parts of the country last century (Punnapra Vayalar in Kerala, the Tebagha movement in Bengal, the Surma Valley struggle in Assam, the Warli uprising in Maharashtra, etc.), the highlight of which was the armed struggle in Telangana, brought the issue of land reforms to centre stage. The consequent abolition of the zamindari system and landed estates drew the vast mass of India's peasantry into the project of building the 'idea of India'. In fact, such struggles contributed the most in liberating crores of people from feudal bondage. This also contributed substantially in creating the 'Indian middle class'.

In today's conditions, the issue of forcible land acquisition has acquired a very dangerous dimension. Amongst the first announcements made by the BJP-led National Democratic Alliance (NDA) government after being sworn in for the second time is the introduction of 'land pooling'. This legalizes the indiscriminate forcible acquisition of agricultural land, dispossessing lakhs of farmers, aggravating the current agrarian distress even further. The question of land, hence, remains a crucial issue for the realization of the 'idea of India'.

Secondly, the Indian left spearheaded the massive popular struggles for the linguistic reorganization of the states in independent

India. It, thus, is chiefly responsible for creating the political map of today's India on reasonably scientific and democratic lines. The struggles for Vishalandhra, Aikya Kerala and Samyukta Maharashtra were led, amongst others, by people who later emerged as communist stalwarts in the country. This paved the way for the integration of many linguistic nationalities that inhabit India, on the basis of equality, into the process of realizing the 'idea of India'.

Even after the linguistic reorganization of states, today, many problems and demands for smaller states keep recurring, reflecting the lack of equality amongst the various ethnic identities that exist in the country, particularly in the north-east. These can only be resolved by ensuring that all the linguistic groups and ethnic national identities are treated equally. This must be accompanied by concrete plans backed by finances, to tackle the economic backwardness of these areas, and to provide equal access and opportunities for all, irrespective of 'caste, creed and sex' as our Constitution declares.

Thirdly, the left's steadfast commitment to secularism was based on the recognition of India's reality. The unity of India with its immense diversity can be maintained only by strengthening the bonds of commonality within this diversity and not by imposing any uniformity upon this diversity. Such imposition of uniformity is precisely what the communal forces are aggressively pursuing today. While strengthening the bonds of commonality is true for all attributes of India's social diversity, it is of critical importance in relation to religion. Following the partition of India and the horrendous communal aftermath, secularism became an inseparable element for the realization of the 'idea of India'. Unfortunately, in practice, however, this went only halfway in meeting the objective of practising secularism as the separation of religion from politics. This means that while the state unflinchingly protects the individual's choice of faith, it shall not profess or prefer any one religion. In practice, this has been reduced to define secularism as equality of all religions. Inherent in this is the inbuilt bias towards the religious faith of the majority. This, in fact, contributes to providing grist to the mill of the communal and fundamentalist forces today. These are illustrative of some attributes of the 'idea of India'. The drawing in of the exploited majority of rural India; the drawing in of the socially oppressed people, especially those who continue to be subjected to obnoxious caste-based oppression and atrocities; the drawing in of the numerous linguistic nationalities; and the drawing in of the multireligious Indian population, and above all, the drawing in of all Indians in an inclusive path of economic and social justice, constituting the core of the inclusionary 'idea of India', remains an unfulfilled agenda. The struggles for realizing these incomplete tasks define the essential agenda to defeat the current aggressive efforts to transform the secular democratic Republic into the RSS project of a rabidly intolerant, fascistic 'Hindu Rashtra'.

A Fascistic Agenda

The RSS's construct of nationalism is its ideological–theoretical justification for the establishment of a 'Hindu Rashtra' (which is distanced from Hinduism as a religion and should actually be called the '*Hindutva* Rashtra'). This is premised on an assertion of the late RSS chief that 'Hindus have been in undisputed and undisturbed possession of this land for over eight or even ten thousand years before the land was invaded by any foreign race'. And, therefore, this land 'came to be known as Hindustan, the land of the Hindus'.[11] It is another matter that historically the word 'Hindustan' was coined by Arabs to describe lands beyond the Sindhu (Indus) River. Phonetically, 'S' becomes 'H' in Arabic.

Hindutva supremacists, having thus 'established' that the Hindus were always and continue to remain a nation on the basis of such an unscientific and ahistorical analysis, proceed to assert the intolerant, theocratic content of such a Hindutva nation:

... The conclusion is unquestionably forced upon us that ... in Hindusthan exists and must needs exist the ancient Hindu nation and nought else but the Hindu Nation. All those not belonging to the national i.e. Hindu Race, Religion, Culture and Language naturally fall out of the pale of real 'National' life.

. . . Consequently only those movements are truly 'National' as aim at re-building, re-vitalizing and emancipating from its present stupor, the Hindu Nation. Those only are nationalist patriots, who, with the aspiration to glorify the Hindu race and nation next to their heart, are prompted into activity and strive to achieve that goal. All others are either traitors and enemies to the National cause, or, to take a charitable view, idiots.[12]

This is in complete contradiction to the 'idea of India' as envisaged by the freedom struggle. Jawaharlal Nehru describes in *The Discovery of India,* 'India is an ancient palimpsest on which layer upon layer of thought and reverie had been inscribed, and yet no succeeding layer had completely hidden or erased what had been written previously.'[13]

Further, Rabindranath Tagore says: 'Aryans and non-Aryans, Dravidians and Chinese, Scythians, Huns, Pathans and Moghuls, all have merged and lost themselves in one body.'[14] And this body is India.

Apart from other dangerous manifestations, which we shall discuss later, for such a regressive project as majoritarian nationalism to succeed in India, central is the RSS–BJP effort to replace history with Hindu mythology, and philosophy with Hindu theology. The BJP government in India is systematically reworking the syllabus taught to our students and youth, and appointing Hindutva ideologues to various key positions in higher education, research institutions and cultural academies.[15]

At a philosophical level, however, the effort is to resurrect irrationalism as the mainstay for the success of such a populist nationalism. Georg Lukács's seminal contribution, *The Destruction of Reason*,[16] in the form of a critique of philosophical irrationalism, needs to be recollected in our Indian context today. Lukács traces, amongst others, Germany's (the birthplace of progressive rationalist philosophy in the nineteenth century) path to Hitler in the realm of philosophy. His central intention asserts 'irrationalism as an international phenomenon in the imperialist world'.

Irrationalism, by its very definition, is an ideological trend hostile to reason. Its main objective, in all its manifestations, from the days of European Enlightenment to today's imperialist globalization, is to challenge the power of reason in human affairs and its capacity to provide knowledge about reality. Knowledge, at any point of time, can never explain the whole reality. However, irrationalism negates the dialectical relationship between reality and knowledge. Objective reality is, as Lukács says, far richer and complex than our knowledge of it. Instead of seeking to bridge this gap on the basis of rationality, irrationalism concludes that one cannot obtain rational knowledge of the entire reality, which can only be grasped with 'faith' or 'intuition', considered a higher form of knowledge. 'Hindutva' feeds people with this idea of 'faith' and, thus, feeds itself to promote its twin objectives of furthering the neo-liberal agenda and transforming India into a fascistic, theocratic state.

Post-truth

The methodology adopted by the RSS–BJP–Modi combine to consolidate the hold of this 'false consciousness' of Hindutva nationalism is through what has come to be termed as 'post-truth'. The Oxford Dictionary declared this term as its 2016 Word of the Year, defining it as 'relating to or denoting circumstances in which objective facts are less influential in shaping public opinion than appeals to emotion and personal belief'.[17]

In the age of Donald Trump and Narendra Modi, it is easy to understand that this term means literally that the truth is left behind and the world is being told to live in false constructs.

The emotional appeals and the building up of a personality cult continuously bombard us with propaganda that India is prospering in a hitherto unknown manner and the only obstacle for creating an Indian El Dorado are the Muslims, Christians, communists and secularists. This is buttressed by intense campaigns for communal polarization and murderous attacks against Dalits and Muslims by the private armies of *gau rakshaks* (cow vigilantes), and moral policing.[18]

Post-truth aims at creating a make-believe world in which people are forced to live and battle on issues based on emotional appeals totally divorced from the miseries of their day-to-day existence. Post-truth, hence, seeks to divert people's attention away from struggles against intensified exploitation and oppression.

The battle against post-truth must be conducted by restoring day-to-day issues of people's livelihood to centre stage.

It is such philosophical irrationalism that permeates all aspects of India's socio-political-cultural life under this RSS–BJP government. This is, simply put, unreason.

Reason versus Unreason

It is reason today to seek the realization of the 'idea of India' by working for an economic agenda that seeks inclusion. It is unreason to implement neo-liberal economic reforms in collaboration with international finance capital that seeks to subjugate the Indian economy to its predatory profit maximization. Such a trajectory vastly widens the gap between the two Indias by impoverishing the poor and enriching the rich. This is an exclusivist agenda as opposed to the inclusive vision of the 'idea of India'.

It is reason today to work for the socio-economic inclusion of the marginalized sections of our people such as Dalits, tribals, religious minorities and women. It is unreason today to promote and patronize their exclusion. It is unreason today to speak of merit divorced from socio-economic realities.

It is reason today to seek 'equality of all citizens irrespective of caste, creed or sex' as our Constitution assures. It is unreason today to deny this equality. Such denial of equality is the consequence of the offensive mounted by Hindutva nationalism.

It is reason today to seek the separation of religion from state. It is unreason today to promote aggressively communal polarization, which promotes exclusiveness instead of nurturing inclusiveness. Such unreason directly attacks the constitutionally guaranteed right to religious minorities, robbing them of security of life and opportunities and making them vulnerable to communal assaults.

It is reason today to foster values promoting the 'idea of India'. It is unreason to poison our education system, in addition to restricting its universal access, through the negation of rationalism and scientific temper. It is unreason to seek the replacement of our rich syncretic culture with Hindu mythology.

The agenda for reclaiming secular democracy means the triumph of reason in this war against unreason. This is the core of the 'idea of India'.

The process of class formation in India, as a consequence of capitalist development, is taking place within the parameters of historically inherited structures of a caste-divided society. It is taking place not by overthrowing pre-capitalist social relations but in compromise with it. This results in the overlapping commonality between the exploited classes and oppressed castes in contemporary India.

Thus, at the level of the superstructure, feudal decadence is combined with capitalist degeneration to produce a situation where a growing criminalization of society coexists and grows in the company of such a social consciousness dominated by caste and communal feelings. Instead of overcoming such a consciousness for the realization of the 'idea of India', it is precisely these elements that are sustained and exploited for political–electoral benefits. Except for the left, in my view, the electoral choices of other political parties are determined by caste, religious and regional considerations.

Current Challenges

What constitutes the essential elements of the agenda that we must adopt to defend and further strengthen the 'idea of India'?

First, this victory and the declarations of the new government clearly indicate that the secular democratic Constitution itself is coming under severe threat. The protection of our constitutional order of secularism from the assault of the 'Hindutva Rashtra' ideology forms the core of the agenda today. The broadest possible unity will have to be forged in defence of secularism and our constitutional order. Needless to add, this can only succeed by sharpening the ideological battle between secularism and communalism.

Second, the process of undermining every single institution and authority under our Constitution is bound to intensify further. It is my own fear that beyond Parliament itself, and perhaps even the judiciary, the Central Bureau of Investigation, the Reserve Bank of India, the Election Commission and all other independent authorities are ever at risk of being co-opted to advance the RSS–BJP agenda. If these august bodies are undermined, it will rob them of their capacity to ensure a course correction against brazen violations.

The undermining of these institutions would permit the RSS to facilitate the transformation of our Republic into a rabidly intolerant, fascistic 'Hindutva Rashtra', which I have been arguing is their aim, consistent with their origins and the reason that Sardar Patel had to ban them as 'forces of hate'.[19] Of special significance is to protect the Indian education system from being communalized to serve the RSS ideological project. The broadest possible unity of all Indian patriots will have to be forged to succeed in defeating these challenges.

Thirdly, the very nature of massive corporate funding to the BJP, and the Modi government's proclamations to collaborate with international finance capital illustrates an aggressive pursuit of neo-liberal economic reforms.[20] This will only worsen the plight of the already beleaguered vast majority of our people. The rich will become richer and the poor poorer. We will have to strengthen peoples' struggles in order to protect the people's livelihood and to force the government to roll back anti-people measures. Once again, the broadest possible unity in defence of people's livelihood will have to be forged.

Fourthly, very big challenges will have to be faced over the democratic rights and liberties of every individual. Already, several incidents of mob lynching, attacking Dalits and minorities are pouring in. This atmosphere of hatred and violence has to be defeated by relentless campaigns against the sharpening of communal polarization. Any expression of dissent or disagreement with the RSS–BJP is slapped as 'sedition'.[21] The Sedition Act, an anachronism in a modern democratic Republic, is routinely invoked for the purpose of silencing the government's critiques. Individuals posting adverse comments on social media are indiscriminately arrested and confined to police custody.[22] The RSS–BJP campaigns against 'urban naxals' and 'tukde-tukde gang' are used to criminalize democratic dissent.[23]

In addition, there are many other aspects that would legitimately be part of this agenda whose final objective would be to consolidate the unity of our diverse people into a single force for creating a better India for our people and for our country by permitting the unfettered unfolding of the 'idea of India'.

This battle will unfold in every single sphere of our social, political and economic life. In the final analysis, it is the people of India who will have to be crucial players in the defence of this idea of India and its full realization.

This can be done only by winning the battle of 'Indian Patriotism' against 'Hindutva Nationalism'.

From the Largest Democracy to the Greatest Democracy

S. Y. Quraishi

Human resources are the most valuable assets the world has.
They are all needed desperately.

—Eleanor Roosevelt

The preamble to the Indian Constitution begins with an emotive phrase, 'We, the people of India', and ends with 'give to ourselves this Constitution'. This implies that the laws of the land and our expectations of the future are not only sourced from the people, but that the 1.37 billion[1] people themselves are the focal point on which all power shall reside at all times to come.

Giving shape to this progressive vision, the architects of modern India strived to ensure that each one of us was accorded equal opportunities to live with dignity and security, with equitable access to a better life, and was an equal partner in the nation's growth. Prime Minister Narendra Modi's slogan 'Sabka saath, sabka vikas, sabka vishwas' (support, development and trust of everyone) symbolizes this original constitutional commitment.

Valuing all people starts with establishing the fundamental political equality of all citizens irrespective of caste, religion, education, economic status or gender. India was a trailblazer in this regard and gave equal voting rights to every Indian citizen irrespective of caste, colour or creed, educational status and especially gender. Why is this unique? This is because it took the USA 144 years to grant equal suffrage to women. The UK, regarded as the mother of modern democracy with its long history of female monarchs, took an entire century of suffragist movement to do the same.

We had a female prime minister within two decades of the adoption of democracy, while the USA has not had a female president in its entire 240-year history. We had the first woman president of the Indian National Congress as early as 1925 when we were British subjects, while it took the UK 300 years before they chose Margaret Thatcher in 1979 as the first woman to head a national political party. Now, who has to learn from whom?

Population Explosion and Brain Drain

In the early decades of independent India, population explosion and brain drain were perceived to be two major curses plaguing the country. People were perceived as a liability, not an asset. To add to it, we were facing an outflow of skilled workforce seeking a better quality of life abroad, which was deemed disastrous for domestic growth and prosperity. Hence, the future of a resource-hungry and overpopulated country losing its skilled manpower was considered bleak.

As we know today, the effects have been quite the contrary. These skilled Indians turned out to be a precious resource that brought us remittances worth trillions over time. The country did continue to make phenomenal progress over the past seven decades. It has today transformed itself from a poor nation into a major regional military, economic and IT superpower. Our population has proved to be an asset, a great human resource.

We have become the fifth largest economy in nominal terms and the third largest in Purchasing Power Parity (PPP) terms, with a GDP (PPP) of $9.45 trillion.[2] We have the sixth largest number of billionaires in the world. The 30 million non-resident Indians (NRIs) and persons of Indian origin (PIOs)[3] dominate Silicon Valley and the world of medicine today. India tops the list of the most remittances received (approx. $79 billion annually[4]), which is a major source of revenue for development. The role of our diaspora is being increasingly recognized as both a source of pride as well as an instrument of soft power.

From the days of Public Law (PL) 480 and a hand-to-mouth existence, India was catapulted into a food surplus country due to the Green Revolution. With pioneering initiatives of visionaries such as Vikram Sarabhai, India reached the moon and is now a major space giant, featuring in the same league as Russia, the USA and China.

All this happened when only a small fraction of our population was fit for employment. Imagine the feats we can achieve if we unleashed the entire nation's human potential?

Manpower: An Indispensable Resource

What is the lesson from all of this? Humans are an asset when strategically developed as a resource. Human resource in a populous country can turn it around if given the space to develop its talents and capabilities. On the other hand, there can be grave consequences if it is allowed to become a liability, which happens if there is a concentration of wealth in the hands of a few, and a lack of quality education.

Unfortunately, income inequality is at an all-time high. An Oxfam Report in 2018 suggested that as much as 73 per cent of all income growth went to the top 1 per cent in the last decade.[5] As many as 70.6 million people continue to live in extreme poverty.[6] Our country is also facing a major crisis of malnutrition, with 50 million stunted and 25.5 million wasted children.[7] This is in stark contrast with more than a million overweight Indian children.[8] As a result of all these issues and many more, we ranked 130 out of 189 countries in the Human Development Index report of 2018.[9]

Hence, my vision for a new India is centred on our comparative advantage in the world—our people.

Who Are the People?

Why should human resource be the focal point of all policymaking? The answer is a no-brainer: a majority of the population is in the working age group (fifteen to sixty-four years) (See Fig. 1). A whopping 65 per cent are below the age of thirty-five. According to a report from the UN Department of Economic and Social Affairs, we will be the world's youngest country in 2020 with a median age of only twenty-nine years. It was recently reported that the world's working-age population has shown the slowest growth in two decades.[10] It follows that while India has a 'fountain of youth', the world is rapidly ageing. Hence, we can become the hub of the global workforce or a huge demographic nightmare, depending on which course we choose to take.

Fig. 1

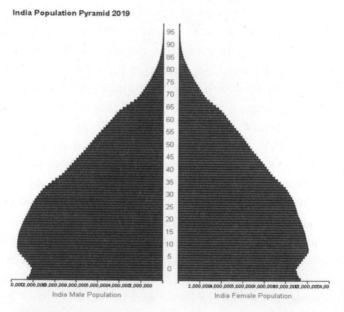

Source: *World Population Review.*

A Window of Opportunity

Why is utilizing our precious human resource so crucial at this point in time? This is because it is either now or never. We only have a narrow window left to utilize the capacities of our working population to the fullest (See Fig. 2). The youth of today will turn into a massive ageing population in as early as two decades, which will be an unmitigated disaster. A prime example is Japan, where more than 28 per cent of the population is older than sixty-five, compared with 21 per cent in Germany, 15 per cent in the USA and only 6 per cent in India.[11]

Fig. 2

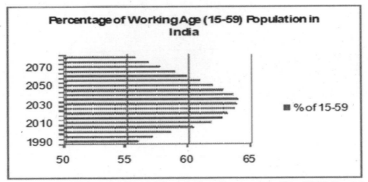

Source: United Nations World Population Prospects—The 2010 Revision

There are a number of downsides to an ageing population (See Fig. 3[12]). First, this leads to a massive economic burden on a shrinking young workforce, as seen from the example of Japan. There are fewer people to work and contribute to the economy. This hurts the productivity of a nation and hence GDP growth. Second, there are fewer people to pay taxes, while more people claim pensions and benefits and other old age assistance. Third, healthcare costs go through the roof. Last, due to the increase in the dependency ratio of the population, there are psychological effects on old people who either live in solitude or are cared for by too few. It is no wonder that China's one-child policy had to be withdrawn in 2015 after thirty-five years.[13]

Fig. 3

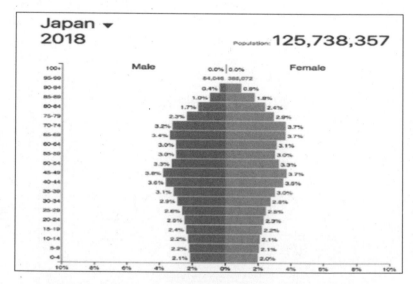

Source: *YC news*.

Equity Is Not Appeasement

In May 2019, at a parliamentary party meeting before the swearing-in, PM Modi remarked, 'We are for the 130 crore people of the country, we cannot differentiate between anyone. We cannot differentiate on the basis of caste and religion or region. We have shown how to achieve sabka saath, sabka vikas (development for all) and now we have to win sabka vishwas (trust of everyone). We are for the people who trusted us and those whose trust we need to win. Nobody should be "other" for us. It takes a lot of strength to try and win the hearts of people.'[14]

These remarks are noble, promising and admirable. The NDA's thumping mandate is yet another opportunity for a radical rethink of public policy for equitable growth. The prime minister has given a vision of inclusive development, which has received admiration internationally. The addition of 'sabka vishwas' further complements the government's vision of not leaving anyone behind.

Development of human resources can only happen when equality of opportunity is ensured. When you fill water in a large pond, the deepest ditches take the most water to fill. Hence to ensure overall inclusive development, targeting the most backward communities is required. This does not mean appeasement. The illustration below brilliantly sums up the value of positive discrimination in favour of disadvantaged communities such as Scheduled Castes (SCs), Scheduled Tribes (STs), backward classes and minorities including the Muslims.

Equality versus Equity

Source: http://www.theinclusionsolution.me/inclusion-journey-rethinking-equity-vs-equality/

It's a grave distortion to perceive equity as 'appeasement'. Uplifting people according to their need is not only logical and commonsensical, it is smart economics.

The Curse of Unemployment

If I could sum up the cause of misery for the Indian masses in one word, it would be unemployment. Half of the working-age population is out of work today.[15] According to the latest statistics, there is now record unemployment in four decades.[16] Even the figures of employment hide gross underemployment.

Unemployment can result from one of two reasons: either the quality of training and education is poor or there is a mismatch between the skills and demand in the job market. While a plethora of causes exists for people out of work, such as the agrarian crisis and stagnation in the manufacturing sector, one major reason is undoubtedly the poor quality of the Indian education system. It has failed to nurture humans as a resource, and continues to produce millions of 'unemployables' (See Table 1). Fake degrees and mass copying in examinations are the rule rather than exceptions. A good example is the field of engineering, where more than 80 per cent of graduates aren't employable, according to a study.[17]

Table 1

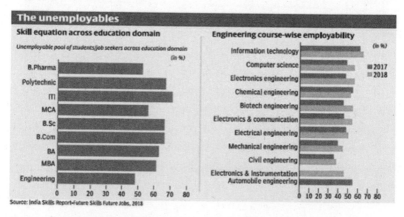

Source: *The Hindu BusinessLine*.[18]

Why is 'work' central to the growth story of any nation? This is because the ripple effects of an unemployed generation are far-reaching. A large unemployed/underemployed population results in a sluggish economy, revenue loss in potential taxation, burden on the welfare system, high burden of disease, poor sanitation, etc. It leads to alienation, frustration, social fragmentation, unrest, mental health issues and criminalization.[19] It is also responsible for the alarming rise in horrific incidents of drug abuse and suicides.

Need for a Paradigm Shift

The National Education Policy 2019[20] proposes some new approaches which need to be debated. There is a famous quote attributed to Albert Einstein: 'Everybody is a genius. But if you judge a fish by its ability to climb a tree, it will live its whole life believing that it is stupid.' Regardless of policies and frameworks, there are some fundamental aspects of the Indian education system that continue to remain a hindrance to gainful learning. For example, the rigidity of our school syllabi where the productivity of extracurricular or co-curricular activities such as sports, music, performing arts and culture have absolutely no value.

There is an extraordinary emphasis on compulsory learning of complex mathematics after middle school, which most children hate. This subject accounts for 90 per cent of their time at the cost of all the other subjects, not to mention the extracurricular activities mentioned above. A similar ratio of parents' money is spent on private tuitions for this one subject alone.

It is but logical that the curriculum must be made relevant to the needs of an ordinary citizen, rather than solely focusing on complex concepts which aren't relevant in everyday life. It is compulsory for our children to learn calculus, trigonometry and algebra, which most will never use in their lives, while these modern Indian 'geniuses' aren't sometimes able to fill simple bank cheques! They are totally ignorant of responsible family life or parenthood. Learning must be gainful, fruitful, useful and interesting, and the students must have ample choices.

Population Management

Despite the population growth rate having declined over the years, India is still growing at 1.02 per cent as of September 2019.[21] We are also set to take over from China the position as the world's most populous country by 2027.[22] The growing population is bound to put an increasing burden on poverty alleviation, food security, education, employment and infrastructure issues. Hence, along with investment in basic public goods such as health and education, we also need a robust population management strategy.

Unfortunately, discussions on population seem to have gone off the political radar altogether. Post the Emergency, when population control was thrust on the nation, leading to a serious backlash, the political class has shown little interest in the issue of population management for sustainable development. What we have instead is poisonous rhetoric aimed at creating a rift between communities. There were very few debates or questions asked on this issue in the legislatures. The department of family welfare was quietly abolished more than a decade ago. This is not a taboo issue, but a prime necessity. A revival of active discussion is essential to ensure that the benefits of economic growth are not neutralized.

How do we manage our human resource to prevent it from turning into a liability? The answer lies in the second stage of life—adolescence (ages thirteen to nineteen)—around which quite a few of our national development issues revolve, such as school enrolment and dropouts, child marriages, unwanted pregnancies, sexually transmitted diseases, child labour, drug abuse, etc. The behaviour and lifestyles learned or adopted during adolescence will influence the health of the individual throughout their lives. Reducing morbidity and mortality among adolescents and improving their development indicators maximizes the nation's opportunity to develop to its full potential.

There is massive attrition in the education system. The dropout rate in classes I to X is around 70 per cent, and only 40 to 60 per cent pass class X and XII examinations.[23] While the age at marriage for illiterate females is fifteen years, it is twenty-two years for women who have completed school. Thirty per cent of adolescents in the age group of fifteen to nineteen years are married. Once out of school, while boys enter the world of work and start worrying about earning, girls suffer the double burden of entering the world of work and also being confronted with matrimony and childbearing. The unmet needs for contraception are also the highest in this age group, with a third having no access.

Coinciding with the International Year of the Youth in 1985, a separate Department of Youth Affairs and Sports was set up and a National Youth Policy was formulated in 2001. The thrust areas for the National Youth Policy include youth empowerment, gender justice, and a multi-sectoral approach to information and research networks. It makes a distinction between the age of adolescence (thirteen to nineteen) and the age of maturity (twenty to thirty). The most important aspect, in my opinion, is that it recognizes adolescents as an age group requiring special attention. It is strange why it doesn't follow the World Health Organization (WHO) definition of adolescence which is ten to nineteen years, depriving millions of young persons between the ages of ten and thirteen of the benefits of any of the schemes.

Although scattered schemes across ministries do cater to adolescents, there is a profound lack of coordination and integration of policies. There is no government policy designed specifically for adolescents. My recommendation is the adoption of a holistic and carefully crafted 'National Adolescent Development Programme' (not just for health) in a mission mode. This must involve an outcome-based approach; monitoring dropout rates from school and learning outcomes; comprehensive and compulsory sex education (or family life education, if that is more palatable); hygiene; nutrition; vocational education; sports; and the needs of the differently abled, etc., targeting adolescents.

The Gender Divide

Dr James Emman Kwegyir Aggrey famously translated an African proverb that said, 'If you educate a man you educate an individual but if you educate a woman you educate a whole nation.'[24] The contribution of women as a human resource is not only as mothers and caregivers but as change-makers within as well as outside the household. Hence, the socio-economic and political empowerment of women is a precursor to an enlightened and skilled society.

But can women be truly liberated in the absence of security? The issue of crime and violence against women seems to be getting uglier by the day. The December 2012 gang rape shook the very conscience of the nation. We did come up with a law after widespread protests, but that proved to be nothing but a knee-jerk reaction unmindful of the root causes of the issue. Nobody uttered a word about society's gender attitudes and structural deprivation that women face in all aspects of their lives inside and outside the household.

No radical rethink has been initiated to inculcate the right values in our children and young people from the very start. At the heart of the problem lies the fact that women are still considered second-class citizens in large swathes of the country. Behavioural change is not and can never be the sole prerogative of the government. The society as a whole must pitch in. Do we ever consciously try to inculcate the right gender attitudes in our sons?

The result is that we see this national humiliation being repeated with sickening and predictable regularity. The gang rape and murder of an eight-year-old girl in Kathua district in Jammu and Kashmir, and the gang rape of a seventeen-year-old girl in Unnao in Uttar Pradesh got special media attention,[25] but such gut-wrenching incidents continue to happen throughout the length and breadth of the country.

A classic case of assault is when disadvantaged rural poor and slum-dwellers go to answer the call of nature, usually at dusk or dawn. Predators are on the prowl to take advantage of their vulnerability.

In 'modern' workplaces, the predatory behaviour of those in power was brought to the fore in the #MeToo movement which highlighted issues related to toxic workplaces. According to a survey of harassment at the workplace conducted by the Indian Bar Association in 2017, as many as 70 per cent women said they did not report sexual harassment by superiors because they feared repercussions.[26] To sum up, women are either forced to unconditionally toe the line or resign. How can India achieve its true potential if half of its population is under constant threat? A National Gender Education Drive needs to be undertaken as part of the efforts to eradicate violence, intimidation and discrimination against our women and girls.

Women need access to education, decent work, equal pay and ownership of assets. We have a lot of work to do as female workforce participation remains an abysmal 26 per cent, down from 36.7 per cent back in 2005.[27] As many as 95 per cent (195 million) of these women are employed in the unorganized sector or in unpaid work.

Due to lack of jobs, men are crowding out women from the workforce in the non-agricultural sector.[28] According to the well-documented crisis in agriculture, men are transitioning to cities in search of job opportunities, leaving women to cultivate the fields. Census 2011 figures show that 65 per cent of the total female workers in India were engaged in agriculture. Out of 144.3 million agricultural labourers, 42.6 per cent were women. But their land ownership is only 15 per cent in north India and about 30 to 35 per cent in south India.[29] Lack of ownership leaves them highly vulnerable to abuse and socio-economic stresses.

As a result of these issues, we rank an abysmal 95 out of 129 countries in the gender inequality index[30] and 149 out of 164 countries on the gender development index.[31]

Reducing the Burden of Disease

A population facing a high burden of preventable diseases will be unable to become a productive force in the economy. In this context, sanitation is one of the most crucial components of preventive healthcare. Even though many policies and programmes were being implemented, the paradigm was never focused on preventive care. India had the dubious distinction of being the country with the highest number of people defecating in the open (a whopping 60 per cent of the world's total until five years back),[32] but the prime minister flagged the issue of sanitation in a number of his election speeches in 2014. After coming to power, he passionately advocated for and heralded the government's flagship Swachh Bharat Abhiyan, one of his best programmes.

Dubbed as one of the largest cleanliness drives in the world, as much as 99.2 per cent of rural India has now been covered under the Swachh Bharat Abhiyan, according to government records. Since October 2014, more than 9.5 crore toilets have been built across the country and 5,64,658 villages have been declared as Open Defecation Free (ODF).[33] A survey conducted between November 2018 and February 2019 by the World Bank covered 92,040 households in 6136 villages across all the states and union territories of India. It concluded that 90.7 per cent of villages declared as ODF were actually ODF, and 96.5 per cent of people who had toilets actually used them.[34]

The Economic Survey 2018–19 also mentioned how the Swachh Bharat Abhiyan, in conjunction with other initiatives such as distribution of mosquito nets, fogging machines and construction of Gambusia fish hatcheries under the National Vector-borne Disease Control Programme, has led to a significant reduction in stillbirths and diarrhoeal and malarial deaths. The provision of safe drinking water, oral rehydration solutions (ORS) and zinc, hand-washing and personal hygiene under the Integrated Action Plan for Prevention and Control of Pneumonia and Diarrhoea are other such initiatives helping to deliver change on the ground.[35]

A National Reconciliation Drive

Prime Minister Narendra Modi's grand vision for a new India has highlighted the need for inclusive development. To realize this vision of progress, growth and trust, it is evident that a developing giant such as India must set its priorities straight. After all, removing socio-economic deprivation can't happen if there are social fragmentations in the society. The obsession with the appeasement narrative must end. Trust deficit among communities is bad news for both harmony as well as economic strength.

India gave the concept of the world being one family ('vasudhaiva kutumbakam') before globalization made the world conscious of it after three millennia. However, negative forces are omnipresent. Racism abroad and casteism/communalism in India are in competition. Communal hostilities have no boundaries. Forces of hatred are raising their ugly head, and the disruptive era of social media along with a mad thirst for TRPs by a commercialized media has aggravated hate-mongering exponentially.[36]

Industrialist Adi Godrej recently warned that economic growth would be seriously affected if 'rising intolerance, social instability, hate crimes, violence against women, moral policing, caste- and religion-based violence and many other sorts of intolerance that are rampant across the country' were not contained.[37] This should ring alarm bells especially because industrialists and large corporations desist from making public comments about society. We must come out of the denial mode.

The uniqueness of this great country is its 3000 years of harmony and intermingling of the races leading to the birth of a composite culture. We have almost all the religions of the world, speaking twenty-two official languages and 22,000 other languages and dialects. My worry is that our unique identity is under severe threat.

Since 2014, a whopping 266 people have been killed by lynch mobs.[38] These incidents of hate and bigotry damage our soft power and diplomatic standing in the world. The absence of intermixing has created ignorance and fear of 'the other' which breeds a vicious cycle of fear, aggression, hate and mental pollution. How will the PM's development agenda be realized if there is severe infighting among the people?

A child growing up in such a society will stop short of being an indispensable resource contributing to national development. After all, 'us' and 'them' are imprinted in their young minds. No child can develop to their full potential if they are brought up as intolerant and misinformed about 'the other'. Development starts with bridging the trust deficit. A national reconciliation drive can be considered in order to ensure that the poisonous election rhetoric doesn't eat into social harmony. Long-term national interest must not be sacrificed for short-term electoral gains.

Reforming the World's Largest Elections

Amartya Sen once said, 'A country doesn't become fit for democracy, it becomes fit through democracy.'[39] In this context, it's an irony that the festival of democracy has become the root cause of the three Cs—communalism, casteism and corruption.

How will we face the enormous challenges and cater to the very diverse needs of our human resource if our political representatives refuse to act in the national interest? In my capacity as a former chief election commissioner (CEC) (2010–12), I find it worth stressing that it is time to take stock of the electoral process. It is frustrating that major electoral reforms have been pending for the past two decades due to political lethargy and inaction.

In this context, the debate on electoral reforms held in the Rajya Sabha on 3 July 2019 was music to my ears.[40] There was a broad agreement on the need for reforms, which is certainly a welcome change. Members of Parliament mentioned a number of electoral reforms that I have been passionately advocating throughout my years in office and after.

Depoliticizing constitutional appointments by appointing election commissioners and the CEC through a broad-based collegium definitely tops the list, especially considering that the Election Commission (EC) was in the dock throughout the election season in 2019 due to a string of avoidable controversies.[41] Removing the role of 'money, media and the mafia' and quid pro quo in politics by introducing state funding of political parties, giving the EC powers to deregister recalcitrant political parties, increasing gender representation in legislatures, introducing some form of a proportional representation for improving the representativeness of the Lok Sabha, etc. are some from a long list of reforms that I have elaborated upon at length at several places.[42]

I don't claim that these measures are quick fixes or politically profitable. But rooting out deeply entrenched flaws needs active political leadership or else all institutions of freedom and democracy will be seriously affected. After all, the ascendant role of money power, paid and fake news, communal polarization and hate rhetoric pose a serious challenge to the very foundations of our electoral system. Until the process of elections is robust, how can we the people prosper?

The government's historic mandate is indeed a great opportunity for reform. At the same time, constitutional bodies themselves have the solemn duty to not allow erosion of their moral authority, which seems to be under considerable stress at present.

The World's Greatest Democracy

To sum up, I believe that the PM's vision—sabka saath, sabka vikas, sabka vishwas—is grand, noble, progressive and achievable. After all, this is a watershed moment in India's history. Not only do we have complex challenges, we are also faced with endless opportunities.

I propose a five-point programme: equity in access to public goods, a national adolescent policy, a gender sensitization drive, a national reconciliation drive, and electoral reforms. My vision is simple: human resource is our comparative advantage and must be treated as the strongest pillar of our productivity and the key to our prosperity.

Being the largest democracy is not good enough, especially when we have the potential to become the greatest. What we need is integrity, focus, coordination, determination and, of course, harmony.

A Shared Past, an Uncertain Future

Syeda Hameed

L et me begin with my story to contextualize my dream called
  India.

To express what has never been spoken, one needs a listener.
No one said this better than my ancestor, the poet Khwaja Altaf
Husain Hali:

Mujhay kehna hai kuchh apni zubaan mein,
Koi mehram nahin milta jahaan mein[1]

I want to say something in my own words.
But I find in this world no confidante

I was a young girl when my father started reciting to me the poems
of Dr Mohammad Iqbal. By the time I was five years old, I had
learnt to read Urdu through the basic primer, and the first verses I
read were Allama Iqbal's poems for children. It was during those
years that I heard father recite lines from Iqbal's poem 'Rama'.
I had read the story of Rama and Sita and enacted scenes from the
Ramayana in school plays. The fact that Iqbal, a poet best known
for writing on Islam and Indian philosophy, should write about

Rama did not appear to me the least odd. In my India, Hindu and Muslim writers often wrote about each other's faiths; that was our eclectic tradition.

Decades later we were 'woken' to face the fact that Rama was a Hindu deity who could be celebrated only by Hindu writers. The other side was equally true: Muslim subjects were now taboo for non-Muslims. For me and many others, it began in 1992 with the demolition of the Babri Masjid, a lesson we all learnt, never to forget.

Thoughts without Boundaries

To go back to the poem 'Rama'. It begins with lines which explain the pre-eminence of Indian philosophical thought over other schools of philosophy:

> *Labrez hai sharab-i-haqiqat se jam-i-hind!*
> *Sab falsafi hain khitta-i-maghrib ke ram-i-hind!*
> *Yeh hindiyon ke fikr-i-falak ras ka hai asar,*
> *Rif 'at mein aasman se bhi ooncha hai baam-i-hind!*[2]

The cup of Hind overflows with the wine of truth.
Philosophers of the West are mesmerized
The high philosophy of Hind's thinkers
Has taken her star to greatest heights

The influence of Indian philosophy over Western thought is a theme that runs through much of Iqbal's poetry. Here he uses it to set the stage for his protagonist, Rama. He ranges Rama along with world philosophers and Imams. This for Iqbal is the highest pinnacle to which a human being can aspire. He compares Rama with *malaks* (angels):

> *Is des men huey hain hazaron malak sarisht,*
> *Mashhoor jinke dam se hai duniya mein nam-i Hind!*

Hai Rama ke wujood pe Hindustan ko naaz,
Ahle nazar samajhte hain usko Imam-i-Hind![3]

This land has fashioned thousands of angels
Who have proclaimed Hind before the world.
The existence of Rama makes Hind proud
The discerning eye sees in him Imam of Hind

Here, Iqbal places Rama in the category of an Imam. An Imam is a spiritual leader; in Shia Islam the best-remembered Imam is the Prophet's grandson Imam Husain. Another fact that is evident in the above lines is that Iqbal holds human beings in higher esteem than angels. Therefore, Rama is presented as a human rather than an angel. In the last part of the poem, he describes the attributes of Rama.

Ejaz us chiragh-e-hidayat ka hai yahi
Raushan tar az sahar hai zamane mein sham-i-hind!
Talwar ka dhani tha, shujaat mein mard tha!
Pakeezgi mein josh-i-mohabbat mein fard tha![4]

The marvel of his guiding lamp
Makes Hind's evening more radiant than its day
Valorous, brave, master swordsman unique!
In purity, in passion, Rama was matchless

The India of my growing years was a space where literature was written without borders and boundaries. I watched poets, writers, activists, playwrights of all faiths come in and out of our home. This *maahaul*, or atmosphere, within my house became ingrained on the slate of my childhood. I grew up on Tagore's words, opening all windows and doors to allow breezes from all corners of the world to waft through.

Another poem of Iqbal's that reinforced the eclecticism of my India was called 'Nanak'. The poet begins by lamenting that we have forgotten the messengers who were born in our land and who began their teachings on our soil.

Quom ne paigham-i-Gautam ki zara parwa na ki,
Qadr pehchani na apne gauhar e yakdana ki,
Ah! badqismat rahe awaz-i-haq se bekhabar,
Ghafil apne phal ki shirini se hota hai shajar![5]

None cared for the message of Buddha,
None recognized the worth of this gem!
Unfortunate people, oblivious of truth,
Like the tree unaware
Of its delectable ripened fruit

Then, speaking of the curse of caste, he makes an impassioned plea. His lines capture the Dalit-Bahujan trauma; words flow from an understanding that transcends barriers.

Ah! Shudar ke liye Hindostan gham-khana hai,
Dard-i-insani se is basti ka dil begana hai!
Barhaman sarshar hai ab tak mai-i-pindar mein,
Sham-'e-Gautam jal rahi hai mehfil-i-aghyar mein![6]

For the lowly Shudra this land is a vale of sorrow;
This basti is indifferent to human suffering.
Still drowned in ego's wine is the Brahmin
While Buddha's flame in foreign lands is lit

In four lines, Iqbal captures the greatest malaise of Indian society. Caste is etched in stone; the Brahmin exults in the wine of his ego while the Shudra's very existence is sorrow. And the lamp of the Buddha illumines foreign climes. The poet then presents Guru Nanak; in this land of ignorance and arrogance, once again, shines a light.

Butkada phir had muddat ke magar raushan hua,
Noor-i-Ibrahim se Aazar ka ghar raushan hua!
Phir uthi akhir sada tawhid ki Punjab se,
Hind ko ek mard-i-kamil ne jagaya khwab se![7]

After an age, once again the temple became radiant;
Aazar's house shone with the glory of Abraham
Once again, the call for God's unity arose from Punjab.
From its dream Hind was awakened by a Perfect Man

Iqbal brings Guru Nanak centre stage. The world is dark, all great teachings have been forgotten here and have migrated to distant lands, and caste is further crushing the oppressed. All of a sudden history repeats itself. Giving the analogy of Prophet Abraham's father, Aazar (a sculptor of idols), in whose house Abraham, the Father of Wahdaniyat (One God) was born. Guru Nanak was thus sent to earth to spread this very wahdaniyat. The soil of Punjab gave the call for unity and India was awakened from its deep slumber by a man who is *kamil* or complete, the Perfect Man, Guru Nanak.

Poetry the Equalizer

The Hindu side of this eclecticism was seen in the month of Muharrum when Muslims mourn the martyrdom of the Prophet's grandson Imam Husain. I recall the dirges and *marsiya*s written and recited by poets such as Anand Narain Mulla and Gopinath Aman. Even today, sixty years after these girlhood memories, tears flow when I hear Muharrum recitation of soz and salaam by Jyoti Swarup Pande, in whose voice the tragedy of Karbala resonates. Verses of Brahm Nath Dutt, a Hussaini Brahmin and frequent visitor to our home, come to mind. As also do the lines from 'Hamd' (Allah's Praise) written by the master poet Tilok Chand Mehroom:

Chaman mein dasht mein vaadi mein koh e sehra mein
Kohar mein, olay mein, shabnam mein, abr o darya mein
Sharar mein, sholay mein, aatish mein, barq e Sina mein
Shamim e gul mein, naseem e masrat afza mein
Ye saray jalway hain kis kay Khuda kay jalway hain[8]

In gardens, valleys, pastures, mountains, deserts
In mists, in hail, in dew, in cloud, in rivers
In flame, in spark, in fire, in the blaze of mount Sinai
In fragrance of flowers in morning breezes
Whose is this radiation? Allah's

And Pandit Daya Shankar 'Naseem'! His *masnavi Gulzar e Naseem* was a treasury of bedtime stories. We listened to *Gul e Bakavali* which featured Prince Taj ul Muluk, Princess Bakavali, and his quest for her treasured 'Gul', the magic rose! The fact that Naseem was a Hindu Brahmin was irrelevant to us children and also to our elders.

This, then, was my India, my secular Divine; no matter what coercion, no one can take away from me the memories of reading Iqbal's 'Rama', 'Nanak' and his poems on the Vedas and Upanishads. Nor can any rightist diatribe erase my memory of the constant flow of non-Muslim poets and writers in our household. For me, they were just *shayars* (poets), *afsana nigars* (writers), and film-makers. The word 'non-Muslims' was not in my dictionary. The gentle voice of my elders had patiently dinned these thoughts into my youthful mind.

I was born in the Kashmir Valley, which today is unrecognizable. It is painful to see its blemished beauty amidst arms, army, boots and terror, as I mourn endlessly for the peace that prevailed at the time of my birth. In 2010 I wrote a poem called 'Mother, I Will Make You Cry Today'. I had read a newspaper report about Asif Rather, age nine, who was accidentally killed by security forces when he ran out of his house to look for his brother Tauqeer. Here is its last stanza:

The crowd stood still
A dozen hands reached out
To hold the falling body
His bullet broken neck
Gently rested on still hands
Of weeping boys
The tousled head of hair
Blood drenched, hung in strands
On a shining forehead . . .

I come from a family which was at once pious and liberal; the word 'pious' then did not carry a negative connotation. We practised all the tenets of Islam, which I also follow every day. As children we were taught the Quran and the namaz, initiated in Ramadan and Muharrum. I was taught Urdu and Farsi before starting formal school. Three lessons underpinned all my education, lessons which remained with me all my life—dignity and equality of men and women, equal respect for all religions, and education as the foundation stone of a good life.

Feminist Upbringing

I also grew up on a diet of the poetry of my great grandfather, who was the first feminist poet of Urdu. His name was Maulana Altaf Husain Hali. Convergence of communal harmony, feminist thought and educational philosophy in his poetry always struck me, even as a child. But it wasn't until many decades later that I realized the relevance of his views in the contemporary world. Hali wrote his first feminist poem, 'Chup ki Daad' (Lament of the Silent), in 1905. His poem 'Bewa ki Munajaat' (Lament of the Widow) was written more than 100 years ago. He was the first to use poetry not as a means of celebrating *gul o bulbul* (romantic love) but to express *hubbul watani* (love for one's motherland) and gender equality.

Talking of *watan*, mine is Panipat, which was at the time a flourishing district of Punjab, with a large population of Muslims. Panipat was the place where caravans of scholars migrated from Afghanistan and Iran to spread their teachings among a populace which was ready and willing to learn. All the schools of Islamic jurisprudence flourished there; people openly debated religion and followed their own *maslak*, each according to his or her light. This town was famous for its Sufi culture, being the *markaz* for Bu Ali Shah Qalandar, known by all as Qalandar Sahib. The distinguishing feature of this erudite, Sufi-dominated town was the primacy of women. Women were greatly revered in my *qasba*. Our homes were known by the name of the woman of the house, for example 'Bi Maimuna ki Haveli' (much later I was pleasantly surprised to see in Marrakesh the same formulation: 'Riad dar Maimuna'). Men usually went away for employment; women looked after the agricultural lands. They went to the fields to collect *lagaan*, driven there in their private *behlis* (bullock carts).

The women and men of Panipat were famous for their *Quirrat* or Quran recitation. The status of women is reflected in the reformist and feminist poetry of Hali. His poems celebrate the woman, not for her beauty but for her grit. Lines of what I regard as women's anthem are:

Ai maon, behnon, beityon duniya ki zeenat tum say hai
Mulkon ki basti ho tumhin, quomon ki izzat tum say hai[9]

O mothers, sisters, daughters
You are the ornaments of the world
You are the life of the nations
The dignity of civilizations

Then there are lines about the deprivation of the rights of women— not only Muslim women, but women of all communities and how the world will one day have to atone for this injustice.

Until you live you are deprived
Of education, learning,
Ignorant you came here, went ignorant from hence
Learning—which for men is the elixir of life
For you it is poison, bitter, lethal and rife
Time for justice draws near
Day of judgment is nigh
The world will have to atone
For depriving you of rights[10]

Today my watan Panipat bears the ignominy of having the worst sex ratio in the country.

In 1947, my mother and other women of the family decided to shed the burqa. Their decision to remove the veil was accepted and respected by the men of my family. These Panipat women were agents of their own fate. When several of these women reached Pakistan (per force they had to migrate), they did not revert to the veil. In either case, no one asked them to wear or remove it; neither the state nor the family.

Partition's Aftermath

Soon after Partition, however, my child-world shattered around me.

When I was nine years old, I had my first direct experience of communal hatred. It was in the aftermath of 1947; several years after blood had been spilt on both sides and wounds were still raw. Parents invariably and perhaps inadvertently passed memories to children. I became the victim of one such 'passing'. In the mid–fifties, we came to Delhi to live in the upmarket Sujan Singh Park; we were probably the only Muslim family in the colony. For some time, I had a secret apprehension that there was something 'wrong' with my name. Whenever an outsider asked, '*Achha, aapka naam?*' I just mumbled hoping there would be no rejoinder. This time I got caught.

Father used to watch me look longingly at children playing in the park. One day he insisted that I join them. 'You will be amazed how many friends you make!' He gently pushed me out. But my instinct proved right. Someone asked my name and that spoilt things; the kids said, 'We won't play with you, you are a Muslim.' 'You have no right to be here; why didn't you go to Pakistan?'

For the next few evenings, I hung out inside the house trying to avoid Father. In my heart, I felt guilty about being in India. We Muslims had asked for a separate homeland and got it, I thought. So why were we still here? I was too embarrassed to ask the elders this troubling question. It was Khushwant Singh who helped me out of my childish anguish. Father and he suggested that I pen this as a story; thus I wrote *You Have to Learn to Make Friends*. How this little book became known the world over is another story, but having made my point I will stop here.

The world around me kept changing for all Indians, especially for the Muslims. After 1947, Indian Muslims took a long time to come out of the fear and insecurity of post-Partition India. Despite the regular communal flare-ups, they began slowly to find their way into the mainstream of life. After Gandhi's assassination, there were mentors such as Jawaharlal Nehru, Maulana Azad, Zakir Husain, Rafi Ahmed Kidwai and educationists such as my father, K.G. Saiyidain, and philosophers such as Syed Abid Husain (who started his journal *Nai Roshni* for this very reason) who took enormous pains to pull them out of the abyss of despair into the new emerging paradigm of the nation.

Seventy years have passed since Partition and sixty years since my brush with its prickly residue. Today, I am older than the school inspector whom I admired in W.B. Yeats's poem, 'Among School Children'. He was referred to as 'Sixty-year-old smiling public man' in a classroom full of kids. I criss-crossed the country for many years going through many 'classrooms' of life. My personal trajectory reads like a storybook. 'Despite' being Muslim I rose to prominent positions— member of the National Commission for Women, the only woman in India's Planning Commission. For thirteen years I walked the length and breadth of this country proud and free, carrying my multiple identities—Indian, Muslim, woman—all cherished within my heart, embedded in every stone, leaf and blade of grass.

The Hindu–Muslim Question

Today, I am recalling all this in the post-election India of 2019. The world has just witnessed yet another lynching in the unending crimes against Muslims. Condoned crimes. I may dwell a little on this because while Tabrez Ansari lies dead in the Saraikela district of Jharkhand,[11] the India of my dreams also lies shattered. A Hindu friend, with whom I share my love for theatre, wrote a piece titled 'Humko Kabhi Maaf Mat Karna, Tabrez' (Never Forgive Us, Tabrez). His Muslim friend had told him, 'This land is no longer for Muslims. We are best off fixing punctures and staying alive.' In July 2019 in Parliament voices were raised against the raging tsunami of Muslim hatred. I watched Tabrez being beaten to a pulp while his glazed pleading eyes looked at his torturers and his bloodied lips mouthed, 'Jai Shri Rama . . . Jai Hanuman.' The crowd watched the lynch game like the hags used to watch the guillotine chop off heads of aristocrats in sixteenth-century France. More words spoken by the crowd were recorded on camera. 'Your name can't be Sonu Ansari. What is your real name? Tabrez? Tabrez Ansari?' My mind rushed back sixty years. 'What's your name . . . don't mumble . . . say your name.' So that is why! Yes, such reactions are why I always used to be secretive about my name!

In 1912, Maulana Azad wrote an article, 'Al Jehad Fi Sabil Al Hurriyat' (Crusade for Freedom)[12] in which he exhorted Muslims to join the Hindus in the fight for freedom. 'Stir yourselves and see; how far the sun has travelled on the horizon. Where have your companions reached and how far behind them are you still lingering? Do not forget what you are; Islam is making its demands on you. How long will your misdeeds pile shame on this Divine Faith? How long will you allow the world to laugh at you and not shed a single tear over your dismal state? How long will the niche of Islam in India remain a gaping hole devoid of its energy?'

Maulana Azad was twenty-two years old when he wrote the above. His weekly journal *Al-Hilal* had created a storm in Kolkata. People were reading the paper and talking in street corners about this firebrand youth. The angrez sarkar was alarmed. Police were dispatched to his home on Ripon Street to seize the paper and destroy the *Al-Hilal* press. The man was placed under house arrest, and to keep him out of the capital he was banished to Ranchi. It was a time of great hardship but he used every moment of his captivity to produce what is undisputedly the best translation and explication of the Quran. It was in Morabadi, Ranchi, where he signed off on his manuscript of *Tarjumanul Quran*. The very same state which has the distinction of being the birthplace of the greatest work on the Quran is also the state where Tabrez and many Muslims were lynched for being followers of the same Quran.

Tabrez's dance of death was performed by one Pappu Mandal to the cheers and applause of many spectators.[13] Could Azad, earliest freedom fighter and profound philosopher, have ever imagined that the country for which he lived and died would sentence his co-religionists to the most gruesome death for the crime of being Muslims?

Many years later, in 1940, as Congress president, Azad spoke at Ramgarh when he defined what it meant to be Muslim in India. He presented his own persona as an example. 'I am a Muslim and profoundly conscious of the fact that I have inherited Islam's glorious traditions of the last thirteen hundred years. I am not prepared to lose even a small part of that legacy . . . I have another deep realisation born out of my life's experience which is strengthened not hindered by the spirit of Islam. I am equally proud of the fact that I am an Indian, an essential part of that indivisible unity of Indian nationhood without which this noble edifice will remain incomplete. I can never give up this sincere claim.'[14] He then went on to define the composite existence of Hindus and Muslims.

This part of the Ramgarh speech I feel should be placed before the nation as a referendum. This Hindu–Muslim question is what the nation must confront today, as a 'yes' or a 'no'.

Eleven centuries have passed by since then [the advent of Islam in India]. Islam has now as valid a claim on this land as Hinduism. If Hinduism has been the religion of its people for several thousand years, Islam too has been its religion for one thousand years. Just as a Hindu can say with pride that he is an Indian and follower of Hinduism, so can a Muslim proudly claim being an Indian and follower of Islam. I could go further and say that an Indian Christian (or the follower of any other religion) can similarly claim with legitimate pride that he is an Indian following one of her many religions.

Eleven hundred years of common history have enriched India with our common creative and constructive achievements. Our languages, our poetry, our literature, our culture, our art, our dress, our manners and customs all bear the stamp of this common life. Our languages were different, but we grew to use a common language; our manners and customs were dissimilar, but they acted and reacted on each other and thus produced a new synthesis. Our old dress may be seen only in pictures of bygone days; no one wears it today. These common riches are the heritage of our common nationality and we do not want to leave them and go back to the times when this adventure of a joint life had not begun. If there are any Hindus among us who desire to bring back the Hindu life of a thousand years ago and more, they are just dreaming and such dreams cannot become real. Likewise, if there are any Muslims who wish to revive their past civilization and culture, which they brought a thousand years ago from Iran and Central Asia, they too, dream and the sooner they wake up the better. These are unnatural fancies which cannot take root in the soil of reality. I am one of those who believe that revivalism may be necessary in religion, but in matters of culture the same revivalism is a denial of progress.

And finally, the clincher:

Our shared life of a thousand years has forged a common nationality. Such moulds cannot be artificially constructed. Nature's hidden anvils shape them over the centuries. The mould has now been cast and destiny has set her seal upon it. Whether we like it or not, we have now become an Indian nation, united and indivisible. No false idea of separatism can break our oneness. We must accept the inexorable logic of facts and apply ourselves to fashioning our future destiny.

In Allama Iqbal's last collection is his eponymous poem 'Pas Che Bayad Kard Ai Aqwam E Sharq?' (What Do We Do Now, O People of the East?) That is my question as well. In other words, what are the disruptive solutions I suggest?

Disruptive Solutions

It is a given that today the words 'Muslim woman' have forcibly been etched on my forehead by the politics of the day. But when I roamed the length and breadth of India my face was unmarked, I was just a woman with the entire sarkar behind me, sent to right the wrongs that had been inflicted on people. My best moments were also my most heart-wrenching ones. All eight states of the north-east—from Mokokchung to Champhai, Sipahijala, Cherrapunji, Churachandpur, Lohit, Kokrajhar and Gangtok—wherever I went I was one with the people. The same held true in the rest of India; there are too many places to name here. Unconsciously, I was following the path of Gandhi when he set out with his lathi and *langot* for the Bharat Yatra.

So, for Muslims and for many Hindus who want Muslims to reclaim their threatened existence in India, this is the only way.

To get out of the comfort of their banal lives and plunge into an India that despite decades of brainwashing still has sensibilities which can be awakened. From sanitized environments get into the mud and muck and be one with the unwashed, unkempt, uncared. As inheritors of the much-maligned Ganga–Jamuni tradition, we Indians in our hearts still recognize our *viraasat* (inheritance) which we will own once the dross falls off.

This is my second disruptive solution. Place before the nation in referendum or whatever form Maulana Azad's words about the place of Muslim women and men in India. Let the rest of the people decide if they are ready to accept the terms that are stated therein. Because Muslims will not live in fear and apology. They need a different kind of oxygen. A population of 180 million will not be wished away. No country will accommodate Muslims if they are forced out of India. The Quran says that there is enough space and opportunity for all on God's earth. Surah e Rahman exhorts human beings again and again not to decry the bounties of Allah:

Fabi aayi illa e rabbikuma tu kazibaan

How many of Allah's bounties will you deny?

Engaging with people from all sections, all those whose hearts beat in tandem, is the only way out of the scenario that is now ready to explode. After all is said, the lines of one Raghupati Sahay, aka Firaq Gorakhpuri, say it all:

Sar zameen e Hind par aqwaam e alam ke Firaq
Kaarvaan aatey gaye Hindostan banta gaya[15]

On the soil of Hind from whole world's quoms
Caravans landed; thus India was made.

The Fate of Shudras in a Buffalo Nation[1]

Kancha Ilaiah Shepherd

This essay revisits the Dalit-Bahujan identity that I constructed in my controversial but well-known book, *Why I Am Not a Hindu*.[2] There is now an urgent need to reimagine the old identity of the Shudra in a new way. To overthrow the Brahmin–Baniya hegemony within the realm of religion, civil society and political society of India, this reimagining of Shudra identity becomes absolutely necessary. Since the Mandal Commission reservation policy came into practice, the top-layer Shudras were excluded from the reserved category. This practice led Shudras to believe that they no longer belonged to the Shudra category and that they were the neo-Kshatriyas of the Hindu religion and society. In my book *Why I Am Not a Hindu*, published in 1996, I described these 'upper' Shudra castes as neo-Kshatriyas, to reflect their hope that Sanskritization would earn them the role and rank in the caste system left largely vacant by the waning of the Kshatriyas, traditionally the second varna.[3]

The varnadharma devised by the Brahmins is fourfold and categorized into Brahmin, Kshatriya, Vaishya and Shudra. Since the time of its inception, the members of the fourth varna, Shudras, have been left on the margins and without equal rights as the other castes in almost all spheres of life. Outside the purview of this fourfold classification, there lies a fifth class considered as untouchable/outcaste, which rechristened itself as Dalit, the broken people. While Dalits and Shudras remain the worst victims of the caste system, Dalits carry the extra burden of stigmatization and violence from their caste superiors.

This power is maintained and stabilized systematically throughout the ages by writings produced by Brahmins such as Kautilya, Manu and the most powerful ideologue of the RSS, M.S. Golwalkar. Golwalkar says that the Hindu nation would be a 'place where a people characterized by Varnas and Ashramas' that would determine its future in the classical mode, that is, to follow the Hindu framework of society, obey the Hindu codes, in short, subscribing to the Hindu religion and culture (the culture of caste) as it operated in classical times. The people of the country must be Hindu by religion and culture and consequently by language to be really included in the concept of *janpad*. This is what constitutes the idea of rashtra to the ancient Hindus.[4] With people whose castes are Brahmin, Baniya and Kshatriya—such as Mohan Bhagwat and Suresh Joshi (Brahmins), Narendra Modi and Amit Shah (Baniyas), Rajnath Singh and Yogi Adityanath (Kshatriya)—in power, it seems quite evident that even at the regional level, Shudras have lost their stance and any power previously procured through feudal landholdings. Their aspiration to transform into neo-Kshatriyas too was extinguished with the rise of the BJP–RSS, since its vision is that of Golwalkar's.

The Hindu Rashtra that the RSS and BJP want to achieve by crystallizing their power in Delhi, in spite of Ambedkarite constitutional institutions in place, is the ancient varna order that could be seen to have become unstable with the rise of Shudra regional rulers. The other central item on the RSS's agenda is the issue of reservation, which they want destroyed by all means.[5]

Unchanging Social and Spiritual Status

Shudras, who constitute the largest social bloc in India, are for the most part removed and isolated from each other and do not seem to recognize a need for collective action at the national level. The Yadavs and Kurmis of Bihar; Yadavs and Jats of Uttar Pradesh; Gujjars of Rajasthan; Shudras of Bengal, who are still outside the bracket of the bhadralok; Patels of Gujarat; Marathas and Kunbis of Maharashtra; Lingayats and Vokkaligas of Karnataka; Nairs and Menons of Kerala; Mudaliars and Nayakars of Tamil Nadu; and the Kammas, Reddys and Velamas of Andhra Pradesh and Telangana constitute the top layer of Shudras. Some of the states and regions constitute Shudra agrarian castes that do not fall under the Mandal Commission reservation policy. And in some other states, Shudras have an absolute disconnect with other Shudra communities, except within their own state and civil society.[6]

Apart from the above-mentioned top layer of Shudras, this category also extends to other backward classes that are listed for reservation in different states of the country. Golwalkar's book *We or Our Nationhood Defined* appears to be mainly against Muslims, but this antagonism does not hinder the spiritual access and equality that Muslims enjoy. Golwalkar violently opposes the rights of the minority Muslim community and also tags its members as 'anti-nationals' for their allegiance to Mecca.[7] While these attacks ask for subservience, they do not necessarily interfere with the internal religious life of Islam, which is a source of egalitarian philosophy. But the larger argument extends to Shudras, wherein they are denied access to Hindu God(s) within the Hindu religious system, since Golwalkar's nation is 'characterized by Varnas and Ashramas'.[8] Following the varnas translates into unlimited spiritual superiority for Brahmins and unmitigated spiritual slavery for Shudras.[9] This is a serious problem that needs critical consideration as spiritual equality is more fundamental and essential than political citizenship rights. Shudras have not had spiritual citizenship rights for centuries and the RSS–BJP is determined to maintain this status quo.[10] Paradoxically, Shudras constitute their main muscle and vote bank. They do not realize that they are burning down their own house.

Even after more than seventy years of independence, the constitutional status given to them as citizens did not contribute to any effective change pertaining to the status of Shudras within the Hindu religion and civil society. This seems to be a result of a passive acceptance of or a failure to recognize their religious subordination and subservience to Brahmins in trade and industry to Baniyas. The Brahmin–Baniya combine of the present day, under RSS–BJP rule, has extensive control over capital and spiritual power. It is believed that this control was achieved, in the ages gone by, through a thorough grasp over the Sanskrit language. This language dynamic helped preserve and maintain the hegemony ingrained in the varna order in ancient times.

With the advent of colonialism and modernity, the English language has now become an instrument of power to employ and maintain hegemony. Shudras have failed to recognize the role of language and the shift in the channels of power from Sanskrit to English, in the past and in the present. The top layer of Shudras was under the belief, particularly after Independence, that they would be the neo-Kshatriyas of India.[11] This belief was a consequence of their being able to acquire feudal landholdings in the princely states, at least for a considerable section of them, during British rule. In the nizam's state, for example, the Reddys and Velamas became feudal landowners and acquired political power through this property.

For as long as India was primarily agrarian, Shudras had some control over the vote base and assumed that they were the real ruling elite or what is sociologically known as the dominant castes.[12] During the early days of Independence, the communist movement mainly targeted these dominant castes by associating them with the borrowed concept of 'feudal lords' without considering the element of caste embedded within Indian feudalism. The outcome of this borrowed concept showed its incoherence when these landowning people never transformed into capitalists, as was the case in Europe.[13]

The Indian capitalist class chiefly constitutes the Baniya or merchant caste and not Shudras. In present times, there are fewer Jat, Gujjar, Patel, Maratha, Reddy, Kamma, Lingayat, Vokkaliga, Mudaliar or Nair industrialists than Baniyas, Marwaris and Brahmins leading and controlling the software industry. The caste–capital nexus became clearer after the BJP came to power— particularly in 2014. Since then, Shudra political hegemony even in the federal states has taken a hard hit. Their belief that they were neo-Kshatriyas has been fading. The association and the strong bond between the RSS and Baniyas resulted in Baniyas becoming the most powerful industrial capitalists, and I believe that the Shudra masses are now being reduced to neo-slaves. Not a single Shudra leader was allowed to become the sarsanghchalak of the RSS, nor did the RSS fight for the priesthood rights of Shudra Hindus.[14]

Spiritual Repression

With already established theological schools and institutions in Hinduism, the RSS has a concealed, effective and well-knit network with all the Shankara peethas and major temples such as Tirupati, Puri Jagannath, Vaishno Devi, and so on. This power over spirituality, like language, operates in a manner that ensures Shudras remain subservient to the Brahmin priestly class and to Baniya capital.

The Hindu spiritual system (integral to electoral operations) has provided no spiritual or philosophical space for Shudras. In Vedic times, Shudras were denied spiritual rights, which included the right to read, write and understand spiritual ideas. They were confined only to tasks such as cattle-grazing and building the meat and milk economy that guaranteed the well-being of the Brahmin, Kshatriya and Vaishya communities.[15] Even in the present capitalist era, this situation has hardly been altered, at least not fundamentally. It only masquerades under modernity in subtler and intangible forms.

Historically, control over God and spirituality was maintained through Sanskrit, which facilitated the Brahmin priestly class with access and communication to God, and at the same time confined Shudras to physical labour. In order to perpetually continue this hegemony, the Brahmin spiritual–intellectual force devised various strategies to keep Shudras under their grip. Shudras have not attempted to weaken this grip of Brahmins and Baniyas even by the beginning of the twenty-first century.

Political power operates under the control of spiritual and philosophical power. Although Shudras had access to state power in some parts of India at various times in history, both in medieval or modern times, under monarchical rule or democratic rule, this did not alter their philosophical and spiritual position. Unless Shudras acquire philosophical and spiritual equality with Brahmins and free themselves from their web of control, they will not be able to emerge from the mediocrity they have been consigned to.

As caste hierarchy is interlinked, the position of Shudras in the spiritual and philosophical realm determines the position of Dalits. The caste system operates in such a way that Brahmin intellectuals, both in spiritual and secular domains, see to it that Dalits are controlled by Shudras. This is a dialectical process of control and liberation. A social force that does not have the ambition to free itself from the clutches of Brahmins in spiritual and philosophical domains would not allow the liberation of other social forces that are inferior to them. Shudras still consider themselves superior to Dalits and Adivasis, and practise untouchability. Dalits, known as the fifth varna, are now fighting a massive battle for liberation. But the liberation of Dalits becomes almost impossible unless Shudras also get liberated in the spiritual and social domains. Political liberation is not enough to liberate people from the clutches of spiritual and social slavery. For all such spiritual slaves spiritual liberation is a necessary condition.

Even if Shudras were to get freed from the psychological slavery of Brahminism, they would not allow Dalit liberation to follow. That is what varna order is.

The same RSS which used to defend the inherited Brahmin priesthood in the name of custom and Agama ordination now makes politically right noises on permitting Shudras into priesthood.[16] In spite of their scattered remarks about supporting non-Brahmin priesthood, their actions always betray their real agenda of re-establishing and safeguarding the varna-based social order.[17] Their proposal for building a centralized Rama temple by demolishing the Babri Masjid is based on their mobilization of Shudras/OBCs repeatedly from 1992. The temple was built by so much Shudra labour as well as sacrifice in the riots, and yet even there Shudras are not allowed to become priests. Even after building the Rama temple with their blood and sweat, their spiritual slavery continues. Brahmin priests will then run the Indian state like the medieval papaldom in Europe and Khalif in the Middle East. Shudras/Dalits and Adivasis will forever be oppressed within this medievalism. Since Brahmins benefit the most in such a system, centralized temples then become tools to stabilize Shudra labour. This process not only excludes Hindu OBCs and Dalits but also rich Shudras. Only when this philosophical position is altered and the spiritual power is taken over by Shudras is any change likely to follow. Philosophy as a major subject got constructed around the idea of God. The state is only a part of that philosophical discourse. Shudras have no say in that philosophical discourse as of now.

If priesthood rights can be accessed by Shudras, the Hindu spiritual system will undergo a revolutionary change. Once the spiritual power shifts into the hands of Shudras—Kammas,

Reddys, Patels, Jats, Gujjars, Yadavs and the entire OBC social force—the Indian education system will also be modified radically. The current system, particularly higher education, even in present times, is under the control of Brahmins. This has had a serious negative effect on Shudra education. Mahatma Phule foresaw this and warned us about the implications of this oppressive system. He exhorted, 'O Shudras! Condemn and banish, once for all, the accursed doctrine of Manu, you will, indeed, be happy, when you take education.'[18] Not many Shudra leaders, intellectuals and activists in subsequent times understood the modern mechanism of Brahminical operation in higher education.

Unfortunately, even a major leader such as Sardar Patel did not recognize this problem, and unlike Ambedkar, he did not propose any roadmap for Shudra transformation. He believed that Hinduism was his own religion more rigidly than Nehru did and did not intend to amend the existing caste relations or its ingrained hierarchies. Nehru was born into a Brahmin family and had got everything that the RSS founder Hedgewar got and more but went against his roots by claiming that in his beliefs he was a 'Buddhist'.[19] He disagreed with Gandhi's Hindu (Baniya) vegetarianism and became a beeferian, inviting the wrath of the RSS.[20] Ironically, it was Patel who gave up on his historical Shudra food culture and turned vegetarian. According to Aakar Patel, most Patels in present times are pure vegetarians who renounced their own historical food culture.[21]

While Gandhi was arguing that the varnadharma system should not be disturbed, effectively implying that the caste hierarchy in Hinduism remain as it is, there was no mark of protest from Patel. Patel's politics betrayed Mahatma Phule and Periyar Ramasamy Nayakar. The BJP–RSS celebrates his 'iron brain' and builds statues in his honour. Unfortunately, he has not written any philosophical text to celebrate his philosophical brain and vision. While Mahatma Gandhi and Jawaharlal Nehru empowered their families and communities, apart from playing a significant role in the independence movement, they wrote their autobiographies by telling their family and personal histories.[22] That became their community history too. Their life stories inspired Brahmins and Baniyas. Unfortunately, Sardar Patel, the tallest leader from the Shudra community, did not write anything. He stuck to the Shudra tradition of not writing. If only he had written about his family and Shudra greatness as being food producers and civilization builders, the status of Indian Shudras today would have been different. While he claimed that he was a Hindu, he never asked for equal spiritual rights. When Ambedkar was fighting for Dalit rights he was working for the promotion of Hinduism, as per which Shudras/OBCs/Dalits do not have equal rights. He did not engage with Ambedkar on the issues of annihilation of caste, maybe because he took Shudra inferiority for granted as it was ordained by Brahminism, and hence the BJP–RSS used/deployed him to tell Shudras that even now they should follow Patel but not Ambedkar. Unfortunately, Shudras do not follow Ambedkar, who worked for their socio-spiritual liberation along with that of Dalits. At many places they participate in attacking Ambedkar statues, and even today live in a philosophy of self-negation like Patel. With this blind following of Hindu Brahminism, Shudras lost a great historical opportunity. Now they have no identity of their own as they were assimilated into Hindu Brahminism during the nationalist period. The BJP–RSS network is using that facelessness of Shudras to continue the hegemony of the Brahmins–Baniyas. It is this iron brain of not only Patel but all Shudras that helped the RSS–BJP come into power. Now there is a dire need for Shudras to acknowledge their position and to fight a far greater battle than Dalits to get out of this neo-slavery.

This movement towards Shudra liberation should be grounded in a scientifically collected caste census that instigates a struggle for reservation. The reservations bloc for Shudras will allow and ensure that the service sector job market of Brahmins, Baniyas and Kshatriyas shrinks. A section of them will have to move into the agrarian production and labour market. Even if a partial section of Brahmins–Baniyas is pushed into the domain of physical labour, their philosophical orientation of life and social relations will alter radically. From this dehumanized position, the process of humanization will begin. Their work in political parties, or secular institutions, outside the domain of basic production has no bearing on social change as the basic hierarchies and caste cultural relations of the production process remain the same. Only a Shudra rebellion against Brahminism can achieve a complete transformation of this situation along with the present Dalit/OBC revolt.

There seems to be a scotoma, a mental block, pervading Shudra civil society that inhibits it from handling any philosophical or spiritual matters. It seems to believe very strongly in its incapability to handle such subjects. This belief and scotoma can only be overcome through education. As mentioned previously, education and language are tools of power that maintain hierarchies in place when denied, but also hold the capacity to transform power structures when provided. It is high time Shudras get out of the Sanskritic social stagnation.

One's access to spiritual and philosophical aspects of Hindu religion also consequently determines their position within national politics. The national politics of India today is completely under the control of Brahmins–Baniyas.[23] The last decade was noted for its decline of the already small OBC share in the Lok Sabha representatives, which continued in the 2019 parliamentary elections. As a representative of this trend, the current Modi government endowed 32 out of 58 ministerial berths to upper-caste persons.[24] As I said earlier, spiritual and educational power is completely under the control of Brahmins, and industrial and business power is under the control of Brahmins and Baniyas. Studies undertaken as recently as 2012 showcase how a mere 4 per cent of corporate board members of the top thousand Indian companies belong to the OBC category. On the other hand, the upper-caste members, particularly Brahmins and Baniyas, hog more than 90 per cent share.[25] In this socio-economic atmosphere, political power at the national level would automatically be under the control of these two communities. That has been the case since Independence. This indicates that not much has changed. The status of a classical Shudra in ancient India was that of a slave. The ancient institutions of religion did not allow Shudras any participation, and the educational and political institutions of the twenty-first century are determined to do the same.[26] Shudras have not yet managed to produce any great intellectuals who could question this oppression, these inequalities and their status as slaves—then and now. They have not realized yet that they remain as unequal as they were in ancient times. The first condition for any social force to fight for equality is the realization of inequality. The second condition then is to acquire the weapons required for the fight.

Primacy of Education

Dalit liberation movements recognize and understand oppression and inequality. They have already acquired the weapons to fight, unlike Shudras. The key weapon in this fight is education. Education provides access to language, which will enable the oppressed to articulate hierarchies and suffering. It also provides a medium to expose the conspiracies hidden within Brahminical structures and institutions. English being a modern language of power has the ability to make explicit and transform the existing domination. Shudras as of now do not realize this and most of them have not attained mastery over this language. On the contrary, Brahmins and Baniyas have recognized its importance and acquired mastery over English, like they did with Sanskrit, to control the spiritual domain.[27]

Historically, Shudras include the agrarian, artisanal and service communities which sustained the Indian economy and facilitated its progress. Their labour force has produced immense wealth over the ages. With time, this Shudra identity dispersed into multiple sub-castes and lost its sense of connection. This being true, none of the Shudra categories were allowed to convert or progress into the Brahmin, Kshatriya or Vaishya category. Although Shudras constitute the largest social bloc and the largest productive community, the lack of cohesion and a sense of the collective has pushed them further into the margins. And the shifts in identity—into different sub-castes—did not help the situation either.

Since the late 1960s, the top-layer landowning Shudras believed and constructed an image that they were not a part of the Shudra community any more. Subsequently, after acquiring power at the regional level, they believed that they were at par with Brahmins and Baniyas. A small section of them advanced into landlordism and local business activities within these regional spaces, which instigated them to project themselves as 'neo-Kshatriyas'. They added all kinds of surnames or titles with this in mind—for example, Singh, Choudary, Patel, Reddy, Rao, Nair, Yadav, Mandal, and so on. These titles gave them a sense of transformation and progress which led them to believe that they were neo-Kshatriyas. However, as neo-Kshatriyas, they have not managed to master a superior tool of power—language—that has a pan-Indian presence. This is quite problematic as the present society does not run on muscle power but on the soft power that is knowledge.

In the modern period, particularly after India achieved independence, Shudras managed to acquire some regional-language education. Their association of education with modernity also supplemented their belief regarding their neo-Kshatriya status. Quite tragically, all these castes only remained as regional power blocs and could not expand further. They could not develop into a national identity the way Brahmins and Baniyas did. Shudras were quite content with the feudal grain treasures and regional power and did not aspire to move into the realm of education, overlooking its importance. Consequently, they never developed a critical bent of mind with inquiry and reasoning, were not exposed to the larger national and global vision, and failed to understand the role of language in relation to power politics.[28]

Caste and Capital

Around the same time, Brahmins and Baniyas were striving to construct a national network—the Brahmin priest in the village associated himself with a national Hindu philosophical centre, and Baniyas established connections with national mercantile/capitalist centres. The RSS established itself as a philosophical centre within their religious domain and the Mumbai-based Baniya capital turned into the business centre. This was not the case with Shudra feudal forces, as they did not aspire for a national collective. They failed to recognize that national political power depends largely on two major pan-Indian structures: caste and capital. Each religious structure has its own national agency and every business class/caste has its own national headquarters. Hence, Shudras remained at the national periphery.

The RSS, which acts as the headquarters of Hinduism, is completely controlled by Brahmins[29] and the capitalist/business economy in Mumbai is controlled by Baniyas.[30] This leaves no space, or rather systematically excludes the participation of other castes, and alienates them from spiritual and economic decision-making. This results from a strong belief that Shudras were exposed to for centuries—that they are slaves. This belief then restrains them from imagining an independent existence and hinders the possibility of mastering the realms of religion and philosophy as they do not deem themselves fit for the task. This belief is historical and continues to operate in modern times in disguised forms, if not in outright explicit ways. The RSS recognizes this limitation of Shudras and deploys it to its own advantage. This has become more evident after the 2014 elections. Shudras voted for the BJP and handed over power to Brahmins, Baniyas and Kshatriyas, very much like it used to happen in the classical form of rule. Shudras used their constitutional right to vote against their own selves.

For instance, this slavish mindset is best represented by the Nair caste of Kerala. Until the early twentieth century, the Nair community allowed its women to live as concubines of Brahmin men in a system called *sambandham*.[31] The Nair women had only the duty of procreating with Brahmin men, but they did not have rights over the Brahmin man's property. The children born in such a sambandham arrangement would not be allowed to become priests and continued to be Shudras. Even though the Nairs did not have any spiritual rights, having been born in sambandham, which is social anathema in itself, they continued to respect such immoral Brahminism and live in self denial. Their spiritual slavery to Brahminism has been revealed several times, the latest being their support to the Brahminical anti-women stand on the Shabarimala temple entry issue.[32] This mindset still persists and operates in multiple ways. The Supreme Court judgment[33] of 2018 regarding the Ayyappa temple instigated the Nair men to force women to protest against entry rights. Their women were made to oppose their own freedom to enter the temple during the menstruating age of ten to fifty years.[34] Hundreds of women were asked to come on to the streets to protest. The belief that menstruating women are impure and that they should not be allowed into the Ayyappa temple was a construct of the Namboodiri Brahmins of Kerala. Shudras had absolutely no role in devising this construct, yet they believed with great conviction that this was true and divine. Not a single Nair emerged as a spiritual philosopher and challenged Brahmins to take over the temple priesthood, nor did they try to alter the codified principles of divine practice. They only implemented what Brahmins codify as spiritual principles. This was true in the past with concubinage and stands true in present times with the temple entry issue.

Shudras were unsuccessful in realizing that mind power controls muscle power. They failed to understand the role of language and education, religion and capital and consequently its influence on philosophical, economic and political spheres. At no point in history have they strived to recognize their own oppression or at least strived to acquire the tools that facilitate this recognition. Shudras only got as far as getting themselves enrolled into RSS Vyayamshalas and not any further. Brahmins and Baniyas, on the other hand, enrolled themselves in Christian English-medium schools as they understood the potential of the English language and education in the postcolonial era of modernity.

History shows that in ancient India, Shudras did not consider it important to master Sanskrit, which had a subcontinental presence. During Muslim rule, particularly during the Mughal period, they did not regard it important to get a Persian-language education. And subsequently, Urdu-language education, which had a pan-Indian presence. Since the colonial period and later, even after Independence, they did not aspire to an English-medium education. On the contrary, they turned into regional-language chauvinists. These castes, therefore, could not produce thinkers who were able to handle national issues or philosophical questions. They never believed in the power of education, instead strongly believing in the power of land and money. This being true, the land and money they acquired were never transformed into capital or used to expand into business.

The neo-Kshatriya titles they acquired such as Reddy, Rao, Patil, Choudary, Yadav, Goud, Nayak, Nair and Mandal (in West Bengal and Bihar) helped them influence and regulate local power. These castes also acquired early local and regional political power after the election system was introduced. The village-level police and revenue power was procured from Brahmins and Muslims (In certain areas such as the nizam's state and Mysore, Muslim zamindari was also strong). Although the top-layer Shudras had police and revenue power at the regional level, this power always remained inferior to spiritual and philosophical power. They never understood the philosophical principle that God controls everything—including the gun.

The regional power acquired by Shudras played a crucial role in the election process. Nehru, particularly, recognized the strength and importance of regional power and promoted some Shudra landlords at the national level who were a part of the nationalist struggles. Sardar Patel, Kamaraj Nadar, Neelam Sanjiva Reddy, Nijalingappa and Y.B. Chavan emerged as national leaders by handling raw politics with some creative ideas, but none of them was successful in handling philosophical, historical and theological questions. Later, although Chaudhary Charan Singh and H.D. Deve Gowda became prime ministers of India for short periods of time, they did not have a philosophical vision which would have allowed them to leave an imprint on the socio-spiritual and political plan of the nation.

The Shudra community did not find a place even within the bureaucratic set-up[35] as they did not deem it important to be educated in English. Not aspiring for good education is a problem of historical location more than a financial matter.

In the bureaucratic set-up, even Shudra/OBC families could not acquire a hold because they had no English-medium education.[36] RTI petitions have revealed that in the cumulative staffing position of twenty-four ministries, twenty-five departments (out of thirty-seven) and eight constitutional bodies, only 14 per cent of Group A officers are from the OBC category. The figures for Group B, C and D employees are 15 per cent, 17 per cent and 18 per cent respectively. In some cases, the under-representation of OBCs is absolute. For instance, in the Cabinet Secretariat, which has sixty-four Group A officers, not one is from the OBC category, while sixty are upper-caste. Even these statistics are just indicative as numerous ministries did not respond to RTI queries regarding the social composition of their staff.[37] It is a known fact they do not occupy top teaching positions in central universities and IIT/ IIMs.[38] They also did not think about the need to put their children into sophisticated English-medium schools and colleges within India and abroad. Historically, there was spiritual opposition for a long time to the education of Shudras, and it became a question of orientation in due course of caste–cultural existence. For example, Brahmins made it a philosophical axiom that the Hindu God should be communicated with only in the Sanskrit language, while simultaneously to handle national and global institutions they sent their children to study in English-medium schools—preferably in Christian convent ones. Putting their children in a suitable educational institution was a matter of philosophical and ideological disposition and not simply a matter of financial adequacy. This was never realized by Shudras in India.

Food Cultures

Even Shudra landlords thought that their children were unsuitable for that kind of educational life. Most of them were uncritical admirers of Gandhi and Nehru and believed themselves to be unable to reach similar national and international stature. Of course, the real cause of such an attitude lay in the caste cultural tradition itself. They carried an intellectual inferiority complex vis-à-vis Brahmins and Baniyas. The image of Gandhi had strengthened the village-level Baniyas. For example, most of the Baniyas, across the country, even at the village level, were vegetarians. They must have got this cultural belief because of their Jain tradition, but Gandhi made it more respectable at a pan-Indian level by taking up a massive campaign linking human food culture and his theory of non-violence. His Baniya vegetarianism was a historically contingent position, but he rendered it philosophically sophisticated to make it seem more ethically legitimate. His campaign made it seem as if Shudras were an inclusive part of the Hindu pure vegetarian tradition. Even Patel seems to have never opposed this kind of anti-Shudra cultural value. As previously stated, Shudras were historically multi-cuisine eaters. But Gandhi gave his family and caste food culture a nationalist twist and projected all meat- or beef-eaters as violent people.

The Gandhian campaign of vegetarianism went well with the north, south and west Indian Brahmins, who had taken to vegetarianism by then. The post-Shankaracharya Brahminism in these regions took to vegetarianism and established it as a spiritually validated theory where vegetarianism was 'pure' and consuming meat was 'impure'. But in reality, the theory was more of an anti-Shudra food cultural theory. Gandhi became the biggest modern nationalist puritan by acquiring a dominant place for Baniyas in modern vegetarian Hinduism. Though spiritual Brahmins had a problem with Gandhi, they accepted his image into their homes very easily with his brand of vegetarian nationalism.

The only Brahmin communities that did not go with that vegetarian ideology were in eastern India.[39] They were fish- and meat-eaters. But they did not contest the Gandhian vegetarian superiority campaign. Despite the fact that the Shudras of India are not vegetarian, they feel ashamed to talk about their historical meat-eating food culture. On the other hand, Muslims and Christians are ghettoized in this environment, and even their universal food culture has been projected as impure.

In this process, some Shudra castes in north India even turned to pure vegetarianism. The Patidars of Gujarat are one such type of converts. Over time, Shudras, Dalits and Adivasis began to be seen as violent, dull-headed people because they ate meat/beef. This aspect of the Baniya–Brahmin discourse not only constructed the Shudra/Dalit/Adivasi communities as violent, but also equated them with Muslims and Christians, who never believed in pure vegetarianism and food-related non-violence. Baniyas and Brahmins projected their caste culture as the Hindu (religious) culture. The RSS–BJP used the same civil societal space to capture power in multiple fields—social, spiritual, political and economic.

Now it wants to impose pure vegetarianism on the whole nation, which I believe is going to weaken it.

Shudras did not understand the implications of leaving everything that was historically theirs and adopting the Brahmin–Baniya culture for themselves, thereby legitimizing it as the national culture. This political blunder and historical amnesia is quite tragic. It is believed that Indian culture and civilization started with the writing of the Rigveda, the text that actually divided Indian society into four varnas. But 1500 years before this text was written, the city of Harappa was built. To build that city, along with other cities, humans used all the artisanal skills that still survive among the Indian Shudra communities. The food culture of Harappans matches with Shudra/Dalit/Adivasi food culture, but not with Brahmin–Baniya food culture.[40] Similarly, there was no notion of pure vegetarianism before the Jain sect emerged in the seventh century BCE. It could be argued that the RSS–BJP, in its attempt to enforce Hindu nationalism in the subcontinent, will render the country a pseudo-Jain nation. If a continuity of historical tradition of India is to be drawn, then it resembles more the present-day Shudra/Dalit/Adivasi lifestyle than anything else. Only recognizing these skills and life philosophies will protect the nation's productive abilities.

The most dangerous aspect of the RSS is its commitment to sustain the classical varnadharma (with Shudras being at the bottom to serve the three varnas above them).[41] That means even if untouchability is abolished, all Dalits will be part of the Shudra varna, with tribals being added to it once this phase of reservations is over. But the Brahmins/Baniyas/Kshatriyas will remain as they are, with all the classical privileges. This is very evident in Golwalkar's thesis.[42]

By invoking Manu, Golwalkar lays down a code, 'All the people of the world will come to Hindustan to learn at the holy feet of the Eldest-born Brahmanas of this land.'[43] In the modern Hindu Rashtra, the status of Brahmins should remain the same as it was in the Vedic period, where Shudras were slaves. If they are expecting the global Christians, Muslims and Buddhists to come to learn at the feet of Hedgewars, Golwalkars, Mohan Bhagwats and so on, one can only imagine the fate that is in store for the Shudras/ Dalits and Adivasis of India in the future.

Feminist Futures and Ideas of Justice for India[1]

Kalpana Kannabiran

'Oh my body, make of me always a man who questions!'

—Frantz Fanon, *Black Skin, White Masks*[2]

At every moment of social upheaval, public debate is torn asunder by the tension between different moral orders and competing moral claims. Without going into the details of articulations that are all too familiar, I will take off from constitutional conversations.

'Constitutional morality' is a term developed during the era of Constitution-making in the 1940s by the Indian philosopher and architect of the Indian Constitution, B.R. Ambedkar, specifically in the context of aggravated and violent discrimination against the castes situated at the bottom of the Hindu social order. Simply stated, it recognizes that the constitutional order may not represent a 'natural' (read 'dominant') sentiment but must nevertheless be cultivated by people across location, even when it directly contradicts their personal beliefs—when such beliefs stand in violation of the letter, text and spirit of the Constitution. Constitutional morality is intrinsic to an idea of justice and the route to transformative and insurgent constitutionalism.

This essay attempts to open out the field of justice through a discussion of its constituents. In triggering a conversation on complex contemporary histories of inequality, violence, discrimination, stigma and exclusion, and the histories of their thwarting through resistance, I focus on courts as discursive sites and constitutional commons where movements and possibilities of constitutional interpretation may converge to produce radically new knowledge, sensibilities and sources of legitimacy rooted in the Ambedkarite idea of constitutional morality.

That said, what are the different layers and axes along which both discrimination and its remedies may be situated? How may we understand the contradictions, contentions and indeed the limits of justice so imagined?

In a society deeply fractured by caste, community, heteronormativity, and strident Hindu nationalism, this is far from easy—utopian even. Yet a search there must be for the fine thread of reason that could help forge a concerted resistance that eschews stigma and violence and encompasses the idea of equality and *queer sororal fraternity* through the sensibilities of an insurgent, transformative constitutionalism.

The Supreme Court of India, in the case of *Navtej Singh Johar vs Union of India*,[3] read down Section 377 of the Indian Penal Code (IPC), decriminalizing sexual relations between consenting adults, irrespective of sexual orientation or gender identity. A process that began with the 2009 judgment of the Delhi High Court in *Naz Foundation vs Government of National Capital Territory (NCT) of Delhi*,[4] this decision, delivered while a curative petition filed by Naz Foundation and other petitioners was pending before the Supreme Court, marked the culmination of the judicial twists and turns in the matter of homosexuality and the rights of queer communities.[5] This campaign for queer rights in courts is the lens through which I examine insurgent constitutionalism, feminist futures and the question of justice.

Sexual identities and practices of embodiment that challenge the heteronorm have had a historical presence on the Indian subcontinent.[6] Transgender persons have also had a presence recognized and regulated by law in India—the recognition was of stigmatized, criminalized practices of embodiment that were subjugated by the state. It is from this position that the transgender subaltern speaks.[7]

The reading down of Section 377 IPC by the five-judge bench is historic for several reasons: gains to do with liberty and freedom on the ground; constitutional interpretation; courtcraft and the uses of emotion, literature and empathy in law; turns in jurisprudence and the use of analogous grounds with far-reaching implications; the creation of courtroom utopias through the deployment of the language of resistance, and a trenchant critique of majoritarianism. Most importantly, however, in this essay, I hope to point to the genealogies of insurgent and transformative constitutionalism in India that this judgment purports to 'inaugurate'—if only to trace an intellectual history of rights on the Indian subcontinent that undergird and anticipate the Constitution, and cut a path through the dense, thorny thickets of 'tradition' towards the rainbows on the horizon. Important as this judgment is, it needs to be situated within the larger discourse of civil and political rights imperilled in the present moment of right-wing Hindu majoritarianism and its dismantling of constitutional regimes at different levels in India today.

Constitutional Lyricism/Lyrical Constitutionalism

In trying to answer the question put to her, 'What use is poetry?', poet Meena Alexander reflects poignantly on the place of poetry in our lifeworlds:

> We might think of history as what is rendered up of the past
> in recorded memory, recorded by those who are in a position
> to do so, having access to the power of public inscription.

But there is an important underground stream of history I have learnt to recognize: secret letters, journals, inscriptions, scribblings on bits of paper smuggled out of prisons. Poetry closer in intent, it seems to me, to this buried stream . . . *takes as its purview what is deeply felt and is essentially unsayable*; that is the paradox on which the poem necessarily turns. A poet uses language as a painter uses color, a primary material out of which to make art. But language that is used all the time and all around us . . . needs to be rinsed free so that it can be used as the stuff of art.[8]

The striking element in *Johar* is precisely the Court's struggle with language—its struggle to find a language that is 'rinsed free' of the accretions of prejudice and the tyranny of the written record that it was deliberating on. Carnivalesque recall of song, ballad, theatre, poetic lament and the performance of public apology help free constitutional interpretation from the shackles of precedent, even while excavating and resurrecting dissents. Although the Court's move is driven by the absolute power it wields over authoritative interpretation (and herein lies the contradiction), the languages of the law, it would seem from a plain reading of this judgment, are inept in expressing the raw emotion of unshackling sexual expression and unburdening the guilt 'history' has imposed on the Constitution. The Court then takes measured, authoritative steps through cases, interpretive hurdles, analogies, sites of memory, dissents, and narrations of lived experience—individual and collective—to decisively rule that Section 377 can no longer be applied to consenting adults.

The literary overtures that provide the invocation in each judgment (Goethe, Shakespeare, Leonard Cohen, Alfred Douglas, Vikram Seth) present a discursive rupture in Constitution-speak from the bench—the literary is spectacular and for a moment when time stands still, the bench, the petitioners, and their counsel stand at the borders together, celebrating being-at-the-borders, as the (shared) defining trait of the radical subject. This lyrical opening of the Constitution unmasks the history of violence visited on queer peoples, both state (including judicially sanctioned violence) and non-state (actors ranging from immediate families and kin to mobs in public places); the violence of incarceration (can we read Alfred Douglas without recalling Oscar Wilde's *The Ballad of Reading Gaol,* and the price he paid for being gay?); the pain of death, and the violence of exclusion, excommunication, profiling, segregation and stigma perpetrated by violent legal regimes for seven decades in the constitutional era.

The play *Contempt* by Danish Sheikh[9] written and performed after *Suresh Kumar Koushal vs Naz Foundation*[10] as also the poem by Vikram Seth (*Through Love's Great Power*), written at the same time, and Justice Leila Seth's calling out of 'judicial pusillanimity' are poignant and memorable inscriptions of the courtroom travails—indeed the *judicial humiliation*—of queer peoples in India and the actual and palpable dangers of the deeply entrenched heteronorm that drives the homophobic blurring of the distinct spaces of court and street.[11]

The continuities between the lyrical constitutional reasoning in *Johar* and similar situations that are analogous at different levels would require a close examination if we are to grasp the full import of this decision. What does violence and loss of liberty do to our lifeworlds? Resistance literatures have shaped the civil liberties and human rights struggles for civil and political rights across the country over decades into the continuing present. Where does poetry (and literature) derive its power from?

'There have been moments in our shared human history in particular parts of the world where poets and also singers have been banned. But why? What is there to fear? Precisely this: the force of the quicksilver self that poetry sets free—desire that can never be bound by laws and legislations. This is the force of the human, the spirit level of our lives,' Alexander writes.[12]

These lines certainly allude to the time Alexander spent in India in the 1970s, and the memory of lives and literatures in peril, but also importantly the power of 'quicksilver selves set free' In 1971, when three revolutionary poets were arrested under the Andhra Pradesh Preventive Detention Act, 1970, arguing in their defence, civil liberties lawyer K.G. Kannabiran forced the court to witness the performance of revolutionary poetry.

'The hearing was totally uninhibited and free. The courtroom was packed and our request to permit the poets to read out the poems impugned by the detention orders was acceded to . . . [T]he best was Cherabandaraju's reading. It was a fine satire on Indira Gandhi's socialism set to rhythm and tune. This device demonstrated the untenability of the detention orders against these three poets.'[13]

These were petitioners under arrest, challenging their incarceration by presenting the possibilities of constitutional utopias to the court in verse. This, then, is but one fragment of the genealogy of the *constitutional lyricism* that is embodied and situated within the particularities of place, cultural politics and history uniquely Indian, urging us to excavate deeper layers of knowledge and reasoning embedded within the intellectual histories of constitutionalism in India. Tracing this genealogy leads us to a different place. It is true that poetry and the literary imagination know no boundaries, and have a peculiarly universal ring even while being rooted in place and marked in time. And yet, the specificities of location enrich and deepen the literary in unfathomable ways. When we consider, for instance, the poetry of the Ambedkari *shahirs* (troubadours) who recited, sang and performed the Constitution of free India even while freedom (and indeed the Constitution) was still in the making, our senses and sensibilities open out to the rich and continuing traditions of Ambedkari *chalwal* (movement) facing the threat of criminalization for singing truth to power:

Know Bhim, ignorant one
It is the majesty of Bhim that has broken the shackles of slavery

Aaji brought home joothan from the village
Never any warm bhakar-bhaji in your home
Your family name, village slave—not the name of your family
Clothes from the dead covered your body
Even so, half covered, half naked
The wealth of the taluk stayed in the treasury
Ajoba walked all the way to pay his dues
The majesty of Bhim brought motor gaadi to your doorstep
Bhim's compassion has made us all Sahabs, Waman
All have become Sahabs, have you been left behind?
Bhim left me saying, 'henceforth you are your own master'[14]

In enacting ways of being human, says Eze, '[n]arratives . . . script human rights'.[15] This reflection on the power and place of the literary in our constitutional imaginary takes us to a long history of resistance against authoritarianism, arbitrary rule and the orders of caste and Brahminical patriarchy ('rules by law') by poets and creative writers in independent India (and also to Wilde, Goethe, Shakespeare and Cohen no doubt). Needless to say, these are sociopolitical and legal regimes premised on the violently enforced norms of what Mario Mieli calls 'genital heterosexuality' and 'educastration'.[16] Through *Johar*, we may interrogate punitive and repressive legal regimes and homophobic social orders that militate against constitutionalism with the ever-present threat of violence, incarceration and criminalization. What turn does this embodiment of the Constitution signal to us in terms of other embodiments and performances of resistance against the repressive hetero–state and hetero–majoritarian regimes? These are compelling questions that must steer courts and people alike to constantly keep sight of their own moral moorings.

The recitation of freedom and dignity in *Johar* foregrounds the centrality of empathy to judicial reasoning.[17] This could, as we saw earlier, involve the recitation of poetry by the client in an attempt to draw the judge into a circle of empathy, just as the expression of judicial empathy could be the recitation of poetry by the bench. Important also, as Justice Stephen Breyer writes, is the capacity of a judge to empathize with those unlike him—for a judge to say quite plainly as he did, 'I'm asking because I don't know'[18]—not merely stay on the side of those who share our lifeworlds:

> . . . [W]hen you are a judge . . . it's important to be able to imagine what other people's lives might be like, lives that your decisions will affect. People who are not only different from you, but also very different from each other . . . And this empathy, this ability to envision the practical consequences on one's contemporaries of a law or a legal decision, seems to me to be a crucial quality in a judge.[19]

Or we could, after Mieli, simply pose the question: Does the recourse to poetry signal the move by the judge to step out towards a homoerotic utopia unfettered by the repressive heteronorm? Is the literary invocation in this instance a necessary condition to be able to *think gay*, both from a personal position of embeddedness within heterosociality and within a hetero-court governed by the 'ideology of heterosexual primacy as simply *natural*'?[20]

There is then a thread between lyricism, emotion and empathy, especially in constitutional jurisprudence around the right to personal liberty, if we were to follow the trajectory of this case. Feminist writing has long challenged the cognitive confinement of sex within procreation under patriarchal heterosexuality. In the words of the inimitable Audre Lorde:

> The erotic is a measure between the beginnings of our sense of self and the chaos of our strongest feelings. It is an internal sense of satisfaction to which, once we have experienced it, we know we can aspire. For having experienced the fullness

of this depth of feeling and recognizing its power, in honor and self-respect we can require no less of ourselves.[21]

The acknowledgement of sexual intimacy and desire—and indeed unfulfilled longing ('the love that dare not speak its name') within court-speak was virtually unheard of prior to *Johar*, where it figures prominently as a measure of judicial empathy. It is not therefore merely in formalistic terms of affirming the right to life and liberty that empathy is expressed. Justice Indu Malhotra, for instance, observes, 'LGBT persons express their sexual orientation in myriad ways. One such way is engagement in intimate sexual acts like those proscribed under Section 377.'[22] Justice Chandrachud challenges the presumption of heternormativity and the standard of procreative sex:

> The existing heteronormative framework—which recognises only sexual relations that conform to social norms—is legitimized by the taint of 'unnaturalness' that Section 377 lends to sexual relations outside this framework . . . Sexual activity between adults and based on consent must be viewed as a 'natural expression' of human sexual competences and sensitivities. *The refusal to accept these acts amounts to a denial of the distinctive human capacities for sensual experience outside of the realm of procreative sex.*[23]

The centrality of judicial empathy in the cluster of cases around Section 377 is also seen through expressions of anger. Justice Leila Seth's sharp response after *Koushal* juxtaposes judicial empathy with judicial pusillanimity:

> The right that makes us human is the right to love. To criminalize the expression of that right is profoundly cruel and inhumane. To acquiesce in such criminalization, or worse, to recriminalize it, is to display the very opposite of

compassion. To show exaggerated deference to a majoritarian Parliament when the matter is one of fundamental rights is to display *judicial pusillanimity*, for there is no doubt, that in the constitutional scheme, it is the judiciary that is the ultimate interpreter.[24]

It is this anger, to echo Lorde, and the fury in the older text in the Satyoshodhak tradition, *Stree Purush Tulana* by Tarabai Shinde (1882)—also importantly the anger in the writings of Jyotirao Phule and Dr Ambedkar—that contain within them a collective vision for a liberating future, and guide action with empathy towards the goal of justice.

However, it is pertinent to ask which citizens/subjects the court deems worthy of empathy, and what may be the differing degrees/intensities of the expression of judicial empathy. If *Johar* is at one end of the continuum of judicial empathy (heightened empathy), which kinds of cases occupy the other end? In the affective conduct of courts, we may clearly distinguish four signposts: judicial empathy on the one end, and on the other, judicial humiliation, judicial pusillanimity and 'jurisprudential dissociation'.[25]

Intersections, Analogies, Resurrections

Naz represents a unique moment in intersectionality jurisprudence, not confined to gender or sexual orientation, and in that single move it is insurgent and therefore transformational.

The insurgent jurisprudence relevant to our present purposes is co-produced by the parties, their lawyers and the bench especially in cases that concern non–discrimination, untouchability and Article 21 rights with the goal of reimagining/reinstating democratic citizenship and deepening radical constitutionalism.[26] Drawing on Dr Ambedkar and Antonio Negri, Upendra Baxi argues that the very idea of the Constitution involves its 'other', namely, constitutional insurgencies—the incessant struggles by the multitude to redefine the terms in which their lifeworlds are organized.[27] It is useful to recall Ranajit Guha's idea of insurgency as

> fundamentally a struggle for justice—the site where . . . two mutually contradictory tendencies . . . that is, a conservative tendency made up of the inherited and uncritically absorbed material of the ruling culture and a radical one oriented towards a practical transformation of the rebel's conditions of existence—[meet] for a decisive trial of strength.[28]

In this context, as K.G. Kannabiran reminds us,[29] the Constitution of India presents us with a break from the tyrannies of colonization and social domination, and Baxi holds out Article 17 as an illustration of the Indian Constitution being a 'tremendous advance from liberal constitutionalism'[30]—a constitutional penal provision addressed to state, civil society and citizen.

The insurgency originates in the refusal of queer peoples to be subjugated under heteronormative regimes that criminalize assertions of gender that do not fit into the repressive regulatory classifications of heterosexual criminal law—oftentimes by sheer persistence in being, becoming and staying queer. And in this, queerness is one of several attributes (for the most part social/collective) subjugated through techniques of control and the exercise of biopower that rein people into intersecting and concentric circles of domination—social, corporeal, economic.

Against this backdrop, analogies present themselves in several hues. The idea of horizontal rights embodied in Article 15(2) and Dr Ambedkar's speech in the Constituent Assembly calling for 'constitutional morality' is invoked in *Naz* for the articulation of non-discrimination on grounds of sexual orientation which is held to be analogous to 'sex'.[31] By the court's argument, this expansive reading of 'sex' enables the construction of prohibited grounds of discrimination beyond 'gender simpliciter' and prevents differential treatment of people who do not conform to 'normal' or 'natural' gender roles.[32]

Babasaheb Ambedkar's references to constitutional morality are of course distinct, emphasizing 'self-restraint, respect for plurality, deference to processes, scepticism about authoritative claims to popular sovereignty, and the concern for an open culture of criticism' as embedded in the core of constitutional forms.[33] His stern reminder to the Constituent Assembly that '[d]emocracy in India is only a top-dressing on an Indian soil, which is essentially undemocratic' harks to the fraught realities of Hindu society broken by caste, where the particularity and pervasiveness of caste defeats the formation of a constitutional culture. In drawing an analogy from this context, not just in the invocation of constitutional morality,[34] but also in the deployment of Article 15(2), both the *Naz* and *Johar* courts set up an excavation of constitutional possibilities through an exploration of intersecting, co-constitutive and analogous performative and corporeal particularities of gender and caste.[35]

This exercise is rooted in the intellectual histories of constitutional insurgencies on the subcontinent and in the continuing activities of Ambedkari chalwal that seek to entrench constitutional morality within popular imaginaries and interrogate public morality in the everyday through micro-practices of resistance and through collective struggle. This is the third analogical aspect contained within this reference to constitutional morality and Article 15(2)— collective resistance as the tool of insurgent constitutionalism. Whether with the poets who recited freedom in the courts during the Emergency, or the Ambedkari shahirs, or queer communities-in-struggle co-inventing constitutional lyricism as jurisprudence, the place of struggles and collective resistance is irreplaceable.

That the intersectional articulation of rights is a method and need not represent a shared outcome or judicial path is evident from the echoes in *Johar* of the decision of the Supreme Court in the troubled case of *Shafin Jahan vs Asokan K.M.*[36] (the Hadiya case), where personal autonomy and the freedom of choice granted in *Shafin Jahan* is reaffirmed for queer persons:

Consensual sexual relationships between adults, based on
the human propensity to experience desire, must be treated
with respect . . . [I]t is important to foster a society where
individuals find the ability for unhindered expression of the
love that they experience towards their partner.[37]

While the question of freedom of choice is one that stretches
between the two cases, the trajectory of the Hadiya case can
scarcely be forgotten—the role of the Kerala High Court in
handing over custody of an adult woman who had gone through
a valid marriage to her father despite her clear objection; the
absorption of the violently majoritarian rhetoric of 'love jihad' by
the Court; the Court's decision to grant custody to the educational
institution rather than permit her to go with her husband in
accordance with her wishes, and the ordering of a probe by
the National Investigation Agency (NIA) into conversions by
the Supreme Court even while it ruled on Hadiya's right to
choice and the validity of her marriage. These facts concerning
the judicial process in *Shafin Jahan* ruptures the seamlessness
of the positive reference in *Johar* to the Hadiya decision, and
marks instead the troubling equivocation with respect to strident
majoritarianism in institutions of justice and national security.
The reference to *Shafin Jahan* needs to be understood in the
context of the string of observations in *Johar* on the urgency of
obstructing the potential damage to the social and constitutional
fabric by majoritarianism.

As the last reference to intersections, Justice Chandrachud, in
Indian Young Lawyers Association vs the State of Kerala (the Sabarimala
case),[38] devotes an entire section to 'Article 17, "Untouchability"
and the notions of purity', where he recalls in painstaking detail the
legislative history of Article 17:

The incorporation of Article 17 into the Constitution is
symbolic of valuing the centuries' old struggle of social

reformers and revolutionaries. It is a move by the Constitution makers to find catharsis in the face of historic horrors. It is an attempt to make reparations to those whose identity was subjugated by society. Article 17 is a revolt against social norms, which subjugated individuals into stigmatised hierarchies. By abolishing 'untouchability', Article 17 protects them from a repetition of history in a free nation.[39]

In tracing the intellectual history of this fundamental right, he recalls the anger of Savitribai Phule, that iconic leader of the anti-caste struggle:

Arise brothers, lowest of low shudras
wake up, arise
Rise and throw off the shackles
put by custom upon us
Brothers, arise and learn . . .

We will educate our children
and teach ourselves as well
We will acquire knowledge
of religion and righteousness
Let the thirst for books and learning
dance in our every vein
Let each one struggle and forever erase
our low-caste stain[40]

Interestingly, in traversing the discourse on untouchability, Justice Chandrachud dwells at length on manual scavenging and on the violence against Dalits in contemporary India—both clearly outside the formal scope of the questions of fact and law before the court, but historic in that this is perhaps a rare, if not the first, judicial acknowledgement of the routine violence of caste orders on Dalits in India today.

The discussion on Dr Ambedkar's *Annihilation of Caste* in *Indian Young Lawyers Association* follows from the delineation of the duty of the court to protect citizens, minorities especially, from majoritarian rule.

Mindful of the historical contexts of these interlinkages between caste, gender, religion and untouchability, the key question is a simple one. Should women be prohibited from entering this temple/place of worship? There is no denying discrimination based on gender—women as a class are barred entry for forty years of their life, extending from minority to late adulthood—and it does not affect men in similar ways. The prohibition is 'pre-constitutional'—sati and untouchability were ancient pre-constitutional customs—and although ancient custom has the force of law, in the constitutional era it must pass the test of manifest arbitrariness. There cannot be, as was held in *Johar* and *Naz*, a presumption of constitutionality for pre-constitutional laws. Tied to this last point is the argument on essential features of a religion—the guarantee of equality extends into 'private' domains of family and community, implicitly and explicitly proscribing structural exclusion or violence within these institutions.[41]

On another track of exclusion and stigmatization, while homosexuality and sodomy were at the centre of Section 377 debates in and out of courts, the transgender question also attracted penalties under this section, in addition to special criminal legislations that targeted transgender persons in unprecedented ways. That the targeting of transgender persons was part of a larger project of colonial regulation and control of the liberty of 'non-compliant' subjects is evident in the inclusion of 'eunuchs' among 'criminal tribes' by the British government, and their regulation in identical ways. There are here multiple levels in which surveillance is embedded for 'eunuchs'—while deportment is one, masculinity in the law is defined as the capacity for heterosexual performance, which has a far wider and loosely constructed ambit. The creation of an environment of revulsion (caused by the *legal* validation of the 'addiction' of certain communities to crime, kidnapping and castration of male children) serves to justify restraints and restrictions by law to be placed on certain bodies constructed as 'other' within the political context of colonization.

In the CTA, we see the coming together of heterosexualization and racialization (racial profiling in fact) that lie at the foundations of the hetero-colonial state in very similar ways with distinct consequences for the large number of groups incarcerated by this law even after its repeal. The attachment of criminality on all communities listed in the CTA continues in the colonial mode under constitutionalism, and herein lies a deep contradiction. The understanding of the erosion of the basic rights of queer peoples therefore interlocks in constitutive ways with the erosion of the rights of other minorities.

At a time when the majoritarian impulse is strident in the public domain in India, perhaps one of the most significant interventions made in *Johar* is the affirming of the rights of minorities. While the application in this specific case is to sexual minorities, taking a leaf from the analogies, extensions and extrapolations—the interpretive strategies—from *Naz* to *Johar*, these statements may reasonably be understood as speaking of minority rights in India in general *from the vantage point of queer rights*. The interlocking between caste orders, majoritarianism and heteronormative regimes produces specific proscriptions of speech and curtailment of liberties not confined to minorities but extending to those who speak with them.

How may we open out the counter-majoritarian tenor in queer jurisprudence to the Article 15 grounds of caste, religion, tribe and sex—in conjunction with each other and severally/separately? And importantly to political dissent?

Baxi's delineation of constitutional renaissance is immediately relevant in drawing together the different strands that interweave into the tapestry of an insurgent and transformative constitutionalism. Constitutional renaissance, he observes so pertinently has a beginning but knows no end because everyday fidelity to the vision, spirit and letter of the Constitution is the supreme obligation of all constitutional beings . . . [A]n 'acceptance of constitutional obligations' [is evident] not just within the text of the Constitution but also its 'silences' . . . Second, courts should adopt that approach to interpretation which 'glorifies the democratic spirit of the Constitution'. 'Reverence' for the Constitution (or constitutionalism) is the essential first step towards constitutional renaissance. Third, people are the true sovereigns, never to be reduced to the servile status of being a subject; rather as beings with rights, they are the source of trust in governance and founts of legitimacy. The relatively autonomous legislative, executive, administrative and adjudicatory powers are legitimate only when placed at the service of constitutional ends. All forms of public power are held in trust. And political power is not an end but a means to constitutional governance.[42]

This also brings to mind Jack Balkin's delineation of constitutional renaissance as consisting of constitutional fidelity, democratic constitutionalism and redemptive constitutionalism.[43] As both Baxi and Balkin suggest in distinct ways in different contexts (and indeed using different lenses), the Constitution is deeply aspirational, and pledging fidelity to the Constitution means working on an incessant 'reawakening' of our society to achieve its ideals of freedom and dignity. In a clear expression of 'redemptive constitutionalism', the resurrection of dissents ('Three Great Dissents' as Justice Rohinton Nariman called them in *Justice K.S. Puttaswamy vs Union of India*[44]) enables the future possibility of a cascading reversal of legislative and judicial derogations of fundamental rights that travel between Articles 14, 15, 17, 19 and 21 importantly, but also other protections in the Constitution. It also enables an appreciation of the value of dissent to constitutionalism—not merely judicial dissent, but dissent by a watchful citizenry (of which the judiciary is part) that educates the judiciary on the meanings of justice and demonstrates the corporeal, political and moral consequences of the loss of rights.

Conclusion

The Supreme Court of India in *Johar* sets up several signposts for an insurgent constitutionalism that bear recall. In the method of interpretation, the garnering of an array of sources from the literary performative to the philosophical (constitutional, feminist, anti-caste, anti-racist, among others) to consolidate and seal an argument on the inviolability of the right to dignity, autonomy, liberty and personhood is perhaps unprecedented in Indian constitutional jurisprudence. Reading Dr Martin Luther King, Jr's *Letter from Birmingham Jail* ('. . . when you are forever fighting a degenerating sense of "nobodyness"—then you will understand why we find it difficult to wait . . .') and with his iconic line 'the arc of the moral universe . . . bends towards justice',[45] the court is seized by a sense of urgency, immediacy and irrevocability of the moment.

The reiteration of the Constitution as a 'living document' (dynamic, vibrant and pragmatic interpretation its hallmark) that guarantees the 'progressive realization of rights' through the doctrines of analogous grounds, 'non-retrogression' and rule of law (as distinct from rule by law), whose primary purpose is the transformation of society, bears infinite recall.

The progressive realization of rights as also the doctrine of non-retrogression in *Johar* affirm equality, non-discrimination, freedom of expression, associational freedoms, shelter, life with dignity, personal liberty and fundamental freedoms, special protections, choice, faith, intimacy, health (full healthcare access and recognition of psychosocial health impacts of criminalization), privacy, sexual privacy and autonomy, among others. Especially for our present purposes, in the light of the resurrection of judicial dissents in *Puttaswamy* and the renewed emphasis on the criticality of autonomy, liberty and dignity in *Johar*, the constitutionality of the claim to liberty and the demand to reject the rule *by* law in *Romila Thapar vs Union of India*,[46] the Bhima Koregaon cases as also the case of Dr G.N. Saibaba[47] spin into view, urging judicial empathy and constitutional lyricism from courts in their reaffirmation of democratic, insurgent constitutionalism.

The courtroom utopias and the intense deliberations on the meanings of constitutional morality that have been the subject of this essay point us towards pathways to historicize law and courts as sites of cultural production.[48] Because of its imbrication in statecraft at this moment of violent and exclusionary nationalism and rule of caste, heightened forms of violence against women, the strident rise of the neo-liberal economy and its constitutive colonizations, the emergence of new official sensibilities on the gender order need to be celebrated while being situated in this larger political economy of disentitlement for we can scarcely forget that '[i]n the gender order as a whole, gendered embodiment establishes relations between changing bodies and changing structures of gender relations'.[49] The disruption of the multisited, standard, heteronormative, binary, legal construction of gender may also be seen as rupturing virulently patriarchal and misogynist statecraft, and is in a manner of speaking the state speaking against itself. In an important sense, these judgments—and the resurrections they craft—are hard-won gains of long-standing movements for women's rights and the rights of sexual minorities, not to speak of the struggles of anti-caste philosophers, workers, free-thinkers and human rights defenders. To extract the fundamental general principle of the right to liberty from the enunciation of women's rights to bodily integrity or the right of transgender persons to personal autonomy, or the right of women with disabilities to reproductive autonomy and dignity, opens out for us the trajectories of democratic constitutionalism that have emerged importantly from a popular understanding of constitutional morality long before it was signposted in *Naz*. The eclectic approach to decriminalizing queer rights that we see in *Johar*—through song, performance, poetry and the outpouring of emotion—bear testimony to the far-reaching influence of peoples' movements on courtroom cultures.

And in the final analysis, we must return to that prescient preceptor of constitutional sensibilities who anticipated the principle of non-retrogression and the need for its reaffirmation and recalibration from time to time to sidestep the perils and pitfalls that majoritarian rule poses to the futures of the Constitution:

> If things go wrong under the new Constitution, the reason will not be that we had a bad Constitution. What we will have to say is that Man was vile.
>
> —Dr B.R. Ambedkar, Constituent Assembly, 1948[50]

Imagining and Embodying the Nation

Navtej Singh Johar

I magining a nation is not independent of how we view imagination itself. Where we find ourselves today, in the face of rising right-wing nationalism, may not entirely be a result of having envisioned wrongly, or exercised our idealisms ineffectively, but perhaps more due to a loss of faith in imagination itself. From my perspective of a Bharatanatyam dancer and a yoga practitioner, I feel that we seem to have progressively confused imagination with projection, and in doing so robbed it of its inherent reciprocity.

Years ago, I turned into an urban activist. Being an embodied practitioner, I have grown an affinity with the body, and was dismayed to see how Indian cities are disrespectful, even contemptuous, of the human body. The human body does not seem to be factored into the plan, design, maintenance or governance of our cities. And the brunt of this contempt is largely borne by the pedestrians, who are mostly the poor and the lesser privileged; the privileged getting whisked through this contemptuous landscape in the safety of their vehicles. This not only points to a marked class distinction between the rich and the poor, but it also reflects the glaring divide between our sense of inside/outside. Inside our homes, most Indians are obsessed with cleanliness and order, at the same time we so willingly submit to the disorder and filth that surrounds us outside, and remain unfazed by perfunctory policies and rules of civil governance. Is it because we are callous and complacent as a people, or does such a divide somewhere suit us?

'Stupid' Matter

Contempt for matter and the body is inherent in our psyches. The philosophy of Vedanta, which can be seen as the predominant Indian philosophy of the time, for instance, is categorically dismissive and abhorrent of both matter and body. It privileges mind over body, thought over action, even idea over lived history. Plus, we are culturalized in comfortably designating the dirty task of dealing with matter, particularly used and discarded matter, to a certain people, be it the woman—the wife, mother, sister or daughter within the family—or the lower classes and castes who are available to serve us. 'I shall throw, and you shall pick up!' seems to be an unspoken dictate that almost each one of us has partaken in in some form or fashion.

The underlying thrust of idealistic Indian theories is that matter does not matter, and that, in fact, it is contaminating. Thus, it advocates, rather rigorously, a separation between lofty ideals and polluting matter. It presupposes the stupidity of matter, viewing it as inanimate and unreciprocal, there to serve a purpose and function, having fulfilled which it must exit into the lower domain of the lesser mortals, who in turn, by the virtue of being matter-handlers, are viewed as not only 'lesser' subjects, but even worthy of contempt, to be kept at the periphery of society. In fact, the exalted status of the haves, the keepers of ideals, morals and propriety, rests precisely upon this marked distancing from the have-nots, the handlers of stupid matter.

Except that matter is not 'stupid', it not only requires respect and responsible handling but it also is actually reciprocal. My understanding of yoga, based on my practice, the study of the *Yoga*

Sutras, and the teachings of my teacher, Sri Desikachar, is that whatever object, image or word that I may choose to focus my attention on, in time, that object—real or fictitious—will begin to reveal itself. Because the very property of attention is reciprocity. It warrants an exchange. And within a resolved exchange lies my sanity, serenity and spirituality.

Today, the world over, we, the ostensibly intelligent and conscious human subjects, have bought into the idea of 'stupid' matter. And we are more the fools for it. Nothing seems to have drawn more contempt than plastic over the last century. It was perhaps viewed as doubly stupid because it was man-made and even emblematic of man's triumph over nature. And today, this same plastic is reciprocating with a vengeance and threatening to destroy our planet. This era, our *yuga*, fears a collapse not due to the wrath of gods, but due to the wrath of unattended plastic.

The environmentalists of course need to be up in arms and ring alarm bells, the activists need to pour out into the streets to protest the production and mishandling of plastic, and the sociologists, educationists, economists and politicians all need to work in their respective fields to counter this crisis. But I really hope that the philosophers start to examine our brand of contempt for matter. This calamitous crisis does not hinge on whether or not to use plastic; in fact, we need to be wary of such polarizations. It actually requires, in the final analysis, our humbling before matter.

An issue, especially one as grave as this, does not need polarizing not only because we are all implicated in it, but more so because polarizing is a deflective construct. It pitches one idea against another and actually often deflects attention from the ground reality, lived history, and the very philosophical paradigm that sustains the glossing over of the real issue at hand. We are polarized over ideas, pushing for the efficacy and correctness of one idea over the other. It is no longer time to be 'correct', but to be open to critique and examine the soundness of our matter-contemptuous ground rules.

Bharatanatyam's 'Fanciful Shift'

The history of Bharatanatyam is fraught with ideas. Almost a century ago, Rukmini Devi initiated the project of saving the temple dance by removing it from the lives and ethos of the devadasis. The devadasis were traditionally both temple dancers as well as courtesans, a combination that neither modernity nor the puritan British could stomach. Annie Besant, the president of the Theosophical Society and the Indian National Congress, and a personal mentor to Devi, most ingeniously offered a resolution to this conflict, nay paradox, by simply reimagining the devadasis; she declared that the devadasis were originally meant to be chaste like the Catholic nuns.[1] And India wholeheartedly bought into this reimagining. It is on the basis of this utterly *fanciful shift* that Bharatanatyam gets constructed. Sheer fancy, then, marks the foundation of Indian classical dance, when lived history and paradox were both self-righteously abandoned in favour of idea. Making fanciful assumptions, fabricating claims, and reimagining history was allowed sanction at that point in our national history, in fact, it became our sociocultural as well as political premise. We must not forget this! Correspondingly, if this essay here is read as proposing a critique of Rukmini Devi, I would like to emphatically state that it is singularly a result of her 'saving' the dance that people like me have been able to become Bharatanatyam dancers. Thus, I cannot but be grateful and indebted to her. And I most deeply am! Thus, it is not Athai's (as Rukmini Devi was fondly addressed by her students) intervention that this essay attempts to criticize, but it tries to point to the political premise that she came to occupy. It is time for us to view the historic unsoundness of this premise. In fact, I would say that the admission of this historic unsoundness at the level of premise would signify a coming-of-age for us as a people and a nation.

In dance, the narrative of the originally chaste devadasi keeps getting denser with every passing generation of dancers. Here I'd like to add that such unsound narratives thrive on polarizations. Because polarization divides attention and deflects attention from the fabricated narrative at the core, it, in fact, serves to protect it. Based on Besant's fabricated 'truth', Devi began by making a clarion call to fellow Indians to step forward and take India back to its pure and illustrious past. She did that by exalting an imagined past while proceeding to extricate the dance from the influence of the devadasis, and then realign it to the text *Natya Shastra*, which was incidentally rediscovered by the British only in the 1850s. The reconstruction spawned many self-aggrandizing narratives, and the glossing over of this *fanciful shift* got woven not only into the pedagogy of the dance, but it keeps getting reinforced through a regular invention of polarizations. Other than the primary polarity surrounding the morality of the devadasi, there emerged the debate around the christening of the reconstructed dance, which was earlier called Sadir. This was followed by the question whether Bharatanatyam ought to adhere to 'text' or if it could accommodate the style and mannerisms of the traditional practitioners, whom Devi viewed as 'vulgar'. In the late 1950s, a heated debate raged between the legendary Balasaraswati, one of the last living devadasis of the time, and Devi, over sringara and bhakti, that is, if the import of the amorous songs of Bharatanatyam was meant to be erotic or devotional. The eighties were a time of social awareness and thus raised the concern of the dance's social relevance, whether it was enough to dance to myths or engage with more socially relevant issues. And then there has also been the ongoing, tireless fight between tradition and modernity.

Today, we stand at the cusp of a new debate around the place of nationalism in dance. These polarities have been reinvented with some regularity; they are potentially exhausting and can force the practitioners, if not also the public, to take sides. But in effect, what these polarizations do is that once again they serve to deflect attention from that *fanciful shift* that lies arrested at the core of this dance. The glossing over of this deceitful shift remains the dharma of dancers today. My firm opinion is that the energy of the dancers becomes so locked, in the deflection of this lie and in holding up the 'pure' stance, that we do not feel able or permitted to somatically engage with the subtleties of our own bodies. In other words, we are rigorously trained to block out the sensory responses of our bodies, because the showing-and-telling of a fixed idea must overrule the aliveness and unpredictability of the material body.

The art of Bharatanatyam then rests upon a textually 'authentic' veneer, but one that cannot accommodate or absorb complexity or paradox—the very stuff of poetry. It remains a dance of platitudes, feigned innocence, supplication and sublimation. Poetry in Indian classical dances is rendered though emotive abhinaya, which could be said to be the art of externalizing interiority, or more correctly, a means of rendering interiority transparent. The interior condition is termed bhava, or feeling. But for this feeling to be externalized, it must have a cause for both its validation and manifestation. For instance, if the selected bhava be sringara, the erotic-amorous sentiment, then I must actively conjure a lover who may effectively cause and elicit my feeling. This conjured cause is the *vibhava*, or one that will make my *bhava vikasit* or allow it to flourish. The artistic challenge is to first carefully script and effectively conjure this vibhava, and then, more importantly, to willingly submit to its influence, the force of its orbit, and its ambiance. Because, the vibhava, like any object, does not come alone, it carries with it its ambiance. And it is its ambiance that I must inhabit to make the poetry and dance come alive. My job is then not to produce poetry, depict the vibhava, or portray the bhava, but to become sensorially available to the vibhava that has a life and force of its own. My intention then is not to dance but to get danced by this imagined, though forcefully real, vibhava; because the very nature of this conjured-up vibhava is reciprocity.

Today, I suspect that we Indian dancers have forgotten that imagination can speak back to us. We have perhaps started to treat imagination in the same manner as we treat objects, lifeless, 'stupid' and devoid of ambiance or reciprocity. And it is due to the fact that our primary preoccupation has been made to become the upholding of an idea, and therefore what we see in dance more often than not is a projection of imagination, that is, imagination that is treated only as a verb and one that needs to be illustrated, as opposed to an abode within which the performer comes to reside and become 'present' to and in the performance.

Cultural Misappropriation

The Sanskrit meaning of asana is 'seat', that is, it is something to be occupied. *Asana dharan kiya jata hai*, asana is to be acquired, pretty much like a guise is donned. It is an extraordinary bodily shape that is voluntarily acquired for the promise of its effects and affects, which in turn may evoke involuntary sensory responses and insights in the practitioner's body and mind. Pretty much how abhinaya initially involves voluntary emoting with the hope that in time, as the vibhava gains life and force, the dance in response to the reciprocal and mercurial vibhava would become reflexive, spontaneous, unstudied, unpremeditated and involuntary, that is, sattvika. Incidentally, the word asana also means 'the frontal portion', which may be presented, offered to strike an interface, or from where the 'driver' may steer and negotiate the space in front. Thus, asana also inherently implies something other than itself, which, like the vibhava, I propose, is reciprocal, and presupposes a sensory correspondence with it.

As I stated earlier in the case of vibhava, each object or shape carries within itself the seed of its unique ambiance. It is within the subtle dimension of ambiance, unseen but palpably sensed, that inanimate objects may exercise animation. And they do so by casting an influence, an affect, a spell. An asana gets stilled and comforted (*sthira* and *sukha,* as Patanjali proposes in the *Yoga Sutras*) when it becomes sufficiently contained within its own ambiance. And this can happen only within the here-and-now, not in a future time when the body may be 'perfected' or become completely emptied of the polluting influences of its corrupt materiality, thereby becoming worthy of the pure ideal, absolute and external (to the body). The experience of being sensorially absorbed in the here-and-now is neither a simulation nor an imagination, and it is most definitely not an idea. In order to arrive at such a state of absorbed containment in the moment, the asana must imbibe an unambitious ease to occupy and accept the shape (as it is!), allow it to radiate its dream for correspondence, and generate its self-containing ambiance. This, to me, is the promise of yoga, and it can happen only when the body has gained the licence to locate its object or ideal within its own materiality.

Asana is thus not a vacant shape, nor does it stand in a vacuum. It carries within it the dream of its ambiance. It is a shape that is alive, responsive, and actively in search of containment. Like the bhava-harbouring body in dance, which dreams of being taken over by the force, prabhava, that is, the affect of its corresponding vibhava, asana too dreams of both occupying and being occupied by the self-affirming containment of its own reciprocating ambiance. It is particularly important to register, at least in the context of embodied practice, that physical shapes contain within themselves the dream of an object, akin to the vibhava, the ambiance of which may perfectly match and validate their subjective condition. Beauty, sukha and rasa lie in the delicate exactness of such a match!

However, we see today that asana is popularly seen as something to be exerted or *produced*, much in the production line mode of good-better-best. It is seen as a self-bettering, self-correcting, moralist and perfectionist practice, where the ideal—be it moral or cosmetic—remains external to the body and looms eternally in the 'bettered' future.

Bharatanatyam too has become a spectacle of self-bettering surrender and supplication. It betrays 'feigned' piety and innocence, and it is for this piety—pure and moral—that it has been chosen to become the prime object of cultural exhibitionism. Such a profound and beautiful art tailor-made to exquisitely address the anxieties of intimacy and the paradoxes of lived life, and to tune into the finest nuances of the body and voice, has been reduced to an instrument of in-your-face, nationalistic projection. Bharatanatyam, today, virtually makes the body absent from the dance. Yoga too fears a similar fate as it has been lately discovered as an object of national heritage. The body in both these embodied national projects must be recruited to proudly and chauvinistically uphold an idea. An idea that will never allow the body to exceed into the richness and subtlety of its own material reality, and thereby it, the idea, supersedes the body.

I have always wondered what chance the embodied practice of yoga has as it gets admixed with body-dismissive Vedanta. Reimagining yoga to be an integral part of Vedanta—considering that Shankara, the most notable eighth-century authority of Advaita Vedanta, categorically dismisses Kapila, Samkhya and by extension yoga in the tenth century—is just as unsound, if not spurious, as Besant's imagining of devadasis to be originally virgins. India's embodied practices of yoga and Bharatanatyam, both of which offer us the promise of an immersive bodily experience, have been nationally yoked to ideas, the former to a matter-dismissive doctrine and the latter to a fabricated history. These are very grave misappropriations, but ones that have remained unaddressed and, in fact, inform us at a very integral level as Indians. If we are in the grip of fundamentalism today, we need to realize that fundamentalism may very well just be the extension of the cultural chauvinism that we have allowed and harboured all along.

Thus, to me, dance and yoga have become interrelated practices, but they have become so because of inquiry, both historical and philosophical. Both share a common history, not only of being embodied practices that stem from the same ethos and the same systems of thought, but also for being singled out as odd, bizarre, and 'shameful' by the British. Inquiry into the history of philosophy clearly tells me that not only did the efficacy of premodern embodied practices in India hinge characteristically on fierce autonomy, but that they have historically been subversive and challenging of the status quo over millennia. Furthermore, it shows that they have been paradoxical, radical and nonconformist, in contrast to the conventions of imposed morality, purity and simplistic theism, which seem to plague the Indian mind within the post-Independence modern period. Another thing that becomes evident to me is that the deeply affirming, pleasurable, empowering, and spiritual mode of self-recognition that both dance and yoga promise is dependent upon the cultivation and 'farming' of after-effects that may arise surprisingly and spontaneously from within an intelligent and sensitively self-regulated embodied practice, and not out of blind and earnest following of instruction and text alone.

Loss of Pluralism

The absolutist dream is not new to India. Supremacists have silently trudged through history amassing believers. Within the subcontinent, we can trace the gradual rise of absolutism and the subsequent erosion, if not obliteration, of plurality through the centuries. A very wide spectrum of plurality—valid schools of thought including the heterodox, orthodox, idealist and materialist, which offered a multitude of varied perspectives on primary concepts such as karma, ahimsa, atman, Brahman, God, vegetarianism, agency, morality, purity are practically lost to us. Today, this plurality has all been morphed or erased out of our consciousness. Vedanta alone remains as the abiding and predominant school of valid thought in popular consciousness; in fact, it has almost become synonymous with Hinduism. Today, in effect, we are left with no other way, than just one, to be Hindu. We have not paid attention to, even overlooked and undermined, our own philosophies, and as a result we are left with one unified Hindu philosophy that offers a 'categorical' version of truth.

The dilemma I mentioned at the start of this essay about practising yoga and Indian classical dance—both of which are considered 'spiritual'—in chauvinistic or fundamentalist times is essentially about practise in times when theism seems to have gained a monopoly. 'Vedanta' in a nutshell can be categorized as a mainstream religion that is conventional in its definition and shares with other world religions the idea of God as Creator, Perpetual Doer or Primary Cause, as well as the authoritative, moralizing judge of merit and demerit. It represents the orthodoxy of the Brahminical order and the preservation of caste purity. According to Vedanta, the phenomenal world is unreal 'because what is real has neither a coming-into-being nor a disappearing. The analysis of the relationship of causality leads to the conclusion that both cause and effect are unreal'.[2] It therefore views the material world as illusionary or contaminated and in opposition to the pure, absolute and eternal Brahman; and defines religiosity as supplication to the 'absolute' and rejection and denial of the material world. Moreover, it considers '[r]ational argument [. . .] incapable of leading to the absolute Brahman, access to which is given only by intimate experience wholly lacking any discursive representation'.[3]

In the fourteenth century CE, Madhavacharya, the fourteenth Jagadguru (pontiff) of the Sringeri Sharada Peetham, put together a doxography called *Sarva-Darsana-Samgraha*, in which the various systems of Indian philosophy were presented in sequence of their theistic efficacy. It lists sixteen philosophical schools, including all the schools that have found mention in this essay—Charvaka, Samkhya, Buddhism, Jainism, Yoga, Shaivism and Pratyabhijna— along with a host of other schools,[4] culminating with Advaita Vedanta as the most evolved option. Somewhere during the subsequent centuries, this grouping is again revised, separating the astikas (believers) from the nastikas (non-believers), excluding the latter as they do not rely upon an idea of God nor the hegemony of the Vedas.

However, apart from the nastikas, a lot of other schools are also sidelined, such as Shaivism and Pratyabhijna, and the revised doxography gets pared down to six. These six—namely Samkhya,

Mimamsa, Nyaya, Vaisheshika, Yoga, and the most perfected, Vedanta—are what students of Indian philosophy today learn as the *shad darsanas*, or the six Indian philosophies that reveal ways of valid seeing. Both these doxographies are clearly drawn from the perspective of Vedanta and directly suggest its superiority over all other schools. Today, however, all the six schools that find mention in the new doxography seem to have morphed into Vedanta. Though the study of all schools must still continue in selective circles, the common man on the street would be hard put to even name most of them. Apart from Buddhism and Jainism, which are still living religions in India, and of course Yoga (which is understood mainly as a regime of physical asanas and not an independent philosophy), the only school that is not only popularly known but seen as synonymous with Hinduism is Vedanta.

The way in which rational, discursive and atheistic ways of seeing have been silenced or co-opted by Vedanta can be attributed to (a) the writing of commentaries on important philosophical texts from the perspective of Vedanta—with every subsequent commentary steering the text to align more with its theistic doctrine, such as in the case of the *Yoga Sutras*; (b) the drawing up of doxographies (which happen to bear tremendous authority in posterity), again from a strictly Vedanta-centric point of view, and then proceeding to categorically nix the nastika schools, going silent on abstract or paradoxical theisms such as Kashmir Shaivism, and effectively reinterpreting the non-theistic, rationalist schools such as Samkhya and others to fall somewhat within the theistic fold; and finally (c) strategically positioning themselves at the four corners of the subcontinent by opening the four powerful mathas, monasteries or centres of learning that also housed libraries, and assigning them with authoritative pontiffs with the aim of propagating and installing Advaita Vedanta[5] as the definitive and most superior doctrine across the subcontinent.

Today, with Vedanta alone being recognized as the all-encompassing school of Hindu thought, unopposed from the inside, the monopolizing theistic project of establishing God or Brahman as unquestionably central to Indian thought is complete. To think of Indian thought within a seriously non-theistic mode of reasoning is almost impossible today; God has come to rule the Indian philosophical stratosphere. The result is that yoga today is popularly postulated as a 'union with God', and Indian classical dance is presented as a means of sublimation or surrender of the atman—lower self or soul—to the Supreme God, Paramatman. To question these models is close to heresy. Indian dance was reconstructed just less than a century ago when it was cleansed of eroticism and thereby liminality, that hinged on the sacred/profane paradox that was integral to it. It has since been presented as categorically spiritual and uncomplicated by paradox. The unwritten agenda of classical dance is to maintain this morally correct, 'representational' stance—which does not allow room for reflexivity of the involution/evolution variety that I described—and offers virtually no scope for the opening up of a self-reflexive space.

A Supremacist Reimagining

Indian dance today is self-endorsing, even self-congratulatory, but it is certainly not self-recognitive. Thus, as a practitioner of these two disciplines, I have embarked on this exercise of deliberately evoking alternative philosophical systems, which have historically countered and challenged the monopolistic-theistic modes of first Vedic and later Vedantic assertions. I am not challenging theism here, but the monopolizing tendencies of theism. Likewise, I am in no way attempting to challenge the highly evolved and profound doctrine of Vedanta, but I certainly wish to point to what seems to be its overarching ambition to silence other points of view. The critical discourse that philosophical pluralism can foster is imperative to not only freedom and autonomy, but also poetry and art. Today, when cultural chauvinism and religious fundamentalism are threatening to scale new and even more monopolistic heights, it is all the more important to evoke pluralism and philosophical discord between valid schools of thought that can and have held each other in check. It can be said that today in India, religion has swallowed the critical discourse of philosophy, and that culture, the classical arts and philosophy have all been reduced to an appendage of religion, whose monopoly depends upon strong-headedly maintaining a philosophical vacuum.

It is not overnight that Indians turned majoritarian and became unsecular or undemocratic. They have just bought into another type of narrative that has been slowly brewing. The supremacists today are evoking and subscribing to that same brand of grandiose 're-imagining' of an illustrious and pure past that we collectively opted for at the onset of our nationhood; the difference is just in the narrative, this time the 'purity' that they are reinforcing is not only moral, but also casteist and communal.

Unfortunately, we have not paid attention to the slow and systemic erasing of plurality on the level of philosophy; not addressed or critiqued the unsound constructions of our national identity; and offered no forums for critiquing fabricated imagination. Our education system, like our cities, has been both uncreative and ungenerous. It has in fact played a part in widening the gap between the haves and the have-nots; our schools and cities have become instrumental in keeping a sizeable mass of the population at arm's length, that is, on the outside. And today, it is these masses that have been democratically harnessed by the supremacist forces into an absolutist narrative.

We have to stop treating select people like objects. And we may be advised to initiate this change by, first and foremost, rigorously reviewing and overturning our disdain towards matter, and by extension those humans we feel have been contaminated by it. Until we don't review this attitude, chances are that our stance towards the ones we have historically othered, whom we consider lesser subjects, will remain, as ever before, patronizing and deeply offensive. We need to clearly register that (a) matter matters and (b) it is reciprocal, and in time it will speak back. And that matter may extend to include all things and beings that we have become conditioned to objectify—be it objects, animals or humans whom we may be loath to fully assign the status of subjects. If we play blind and mute to the reality of matter, and choose to continue with our polarized battles over lofty ideals, it will strike back. Because neither it, nor those contaminated by it, are stupid. And if we don't pay attention to and view them as worthy of exchange, they shall in time and turn stupefy us. And most deservedly so!

The Battle for India's Soul

Pushparaj Deshpande

Like all nations, India is a bold adventure of ideas. It is a laboratory of dreams and leaps of faith. Stemming from the experiences of the freedom struggle, the founders of modern India imagined a nation that marked a radical departure from the 'graded inequality' of the past. In doing so, they consciously used divergent approaches and multiple ideas of India to forge a nation that was more than their individual dreams. The visionary charter they crafted guaranteed socio-economic equality for all (the right to equality, and right against exploitation), religious tolerance and secularism (the right to freedom of religion), and equally important, the right to live with human dignity. The underlying principles of this shared dream, that we today know as the constitutional idea of India, are that each person was accorded equal opportunity to live with dignity and security, had equitable access to a better life, and was an equal partner in the nation's growth. This forms the underlying basis of who we are, and who we can be.

It is seldom recognized that this dream was extremely radical for its time considering the historical trajectories of countries such as the USA, and most countries in Europe. African Americans and Native

Americans in the USA won these freedoms almost two centuries after the declaration of independence. Similarly, Jews and ethnic minorities (and even Indians) were treated as subhuman for centuries throughout Europe, as were Black African, Coloured and Asian Africans in south and south-west Africa. In stark contrast, India's founders consciously imagined a nation different from what they saw. Surrounded by wars and authoritarianism, they chose non-violence and democracy. Faced with exclusionary citizenship, they opted for universal enfranchisement and inclusive development. Experiencing oppression, they opted for equality. That quest, to always choose what is best for the people, defines our republic. It is because of that quest that India became a beacon of hope and inspiration the world over.

Challenges to Forging a Nation

It is largely because of this shared dream that India was able to belie the pervasive scepticism about its survivability. Winston Churchill had infamously argued,[1] 'In handing over the Government of India to these so-called political classes we are handing over to men of straw, of whom, in a few years, no trace will remain.' Similarly, scholar–journalist Selig S. Harrison had posited that 'the odds are almost wholly against the survival of freedom and . . . the issue is, in fact, whether any Indian state can survive at all'.[2] They and others had good reason to be sceptical. After a lifetime of colonial exploitation, India had been reduced to one of the poorest nations in the world. Largely because some $44.6 trillion was systematically siphoned away from India between 1765 and 1938, the average standard of living in India had stagnated since about 1890, and nearly two in three Indians lived in poverty.

Despite these formidable challenges, India made substantial strides forward. Consider these:

1. In 1951, India's GDP was 2.9 per cent. By 2010, this had risen to 10.55 per cent.[3]

2. Producing just 50.8 million tonnes, India was a net importer of foodgrains in 1950. By 2012, India produced a record 257.4 million tonnes of foodgrains (and had become a net exporter).[4]

3. The number of schools in India increased from 7416 in 1950 to 3.9 lakh schools in 2013. Consequently, the literacy rate jumped from 18.3 per cent to 74.04 per cent.[5]

4. Similarly, the number of higher educational institutions increased from thirty-five universities and 700 colleges in 1950 to 700 universities and 35,000 colleges in 2012. Consequently, while only 1 lakh students had access to higher education then, over 25 million have access to higher education today.[6]

5. From the 1362 MW installed power capacity in 1947, India boasted of 2.33 lakh MW IN 2017.[7]

6. As compared to the 4 lakh km of roads in 1950, India had 46.9 lakh km of roads by 2012.[8]

7. Finally, India's exports in 1950 amounted to only $1269 million. By 2012, they had jumped to $3.04 lakh million.[9]

Undoubtedly, with some notable exceptions, the makers of modern India did manage to forge a nation in these past seventy years. This was especially impressive given that with all her diversity, building India has always been a challenging adventure. People have always subscribed to overlapping religious, regional, caste, gender, linguistic and ideological identities, which have been at odds with each other for centuries.

And yet, it is these very cleavages that have simmered just beneath the nation's consciousness. Appearing in spurts only when it boils over, this has been a civilizational fight between differing ideas of India—between what was, what is, and most of all, about what should be.

India forgot Dr B.R. Ambedkar's prescient argument that 'rights are protected not by law but by social and moral conscience of the society. If social conscience is such that it is prepared to recognize the rights which law proposes to enact, rights will be safe and secure. But *if the fundamental rights are opposed by the community, no Law, no Parliament, no Judiciary can guarantee them in the real sense of the word*.[10] In India, there exists a *law of the land*, which the Constituent Assembly and later various governments spearheaded and implemented (with varying degrees of success). The bitter reality, however, is that covertly resisting and opposing this supra framework are various dominant communities and organizations (who also dominate the state apparatus responsible for the implementation of the law of the land), who religiously adhere to the *laws in the land*, which are sometimes diagrammatically opposed to the norms enshrined in the Constitution of India. And therein lies the real problem that we face today. It is because constitutional principles are not deeply embedded in the collective consciousness of India that regressive organizations have been able to instrumentally exploit communal, casteist, regional and linguistic disunities for their ideological and political agendas. Today, for the first time since India's independence, it appears that we are at war with ourselves, in which there are no defined sides, and the traditional champions of each side turn easily.

The consequences of this war include the collapse of the political centre coupled with extreme polarization between the left and the right, institutional atrophy, exacerbation of majoritarian and centrifugal tendencies that threaten the sovereignty of the nation-state, and concurrent centralization of power by authoritarian forces.

With the collapse of the political centre, politics in India has become so gladiatorial and performance-oriented that truth has been reduced to a mere prop. The left and right, as well as experts-for-hire (with varying levels of credibility), have aggressively propagated divergent 'facts' that pander to the prejudices of the parties' core bases. These inevitably obfuscate reality and reduce the complexities of real life to binaries. Nearly every medium, be it the media (electronic and print), social media (platforms and messaging services) and forums for political debate (Parliament, press conferences, rallies, etc.) have all been appropriated to amplify these binaries. With so much conflicting information, public opinion has swung like a pendulum from one binary to another.

At the same time, there is a sneaking suspicion that India's political institutions and government policies are driven by partisan agendas. This negates the bipartisan consensus on the fundamental role of the state, which was to serve as a neutral arbitrator between diverse interests. Rather than dispassionately negotiating with and managing a plethora of interests, which is how the Indian state managed to establish itself as the penultimate custodian of order over the past seventy years, the state apparatus is reportedly being appropriated to suppress India's constituent units into accepting one ideology and one leader. Parliament, the media, the bureaucracy, the Election Commission, the police and almost every institution by which the state stood its ground in the last seventy years is either being ambushed or hijacked to further this cause.

Reconceptualizing the Citizen's Relationship with the State

This has led to a dramatic reconceptualization of the citizen's relationship with the state. Given India's founders envisioned India as a social democracy, they saw the government's primary duty as guaranteeing and delivering those conditions that would actualize fullness of life for every citizen regardless of their caste, gender, religion or class. This included guaranteeing social rights (access to the basic conditions of life such as health, primary education, food, shelter and work) as well as political, civil and cultural rights (freedoms of speech, expression, association and religion). Today it appears that India is straying from this consensus (and evidence, both anecdotal and empirical, suggests we already have).

On the one hand, rather than viewing citizens as *holders of inalienable rights*, the state is increasingly viewing citizens as *consumers of government services*. The rights of citizens are being redefined in terms of 'choice' between competing services, and the only real choice a citizen has is to 'walk away' from a service provider. Here, the nature and extent of a government's engagement (vis-à-vis citizens) is also determined by market forces. Based on the logic of the market, the state is increasingly reserving the right to withdraw its services, or outsourcing the delivery of public services to private suppliers. This process has been coupled with radical cuts in social sector expenditure, and the systematic undermining of existing welfare programmes.[11]

On the other hand, political, civil and cultural rights of citizens are being methodically undermined, like in Venezuela[12] and the Philippines.[13] Rigid norms are being imposed with regard to food, clothing, language, mobility, religion and free speech. It is a matter of record that religion is being weaponized in this endeavour, as has been the case in Hungary,[14] India[15] and Myanmar.[16] In doing so, at least with regard to India, Hinduism is being reduced into a prison for those within, a justification for targeting those outside, and is being cynically misused to consolidate privileges (religious and caste based) and secure electoral victories. To borrow from Rohith Vemula, today the 'value of a man [has been] reduced to his immediate identity and nearest possibility. To a vote. To a number. To a thing. Never [is] a man treated as a mind. As a glorious thing'.[17] This poses a grave threat to India's inclusive conception of polity and citizenship.

It is not only the state that is imposing these norms. Private militias have been allowed to violently impose regressive norms on Scheduled Castes (Dalits), Scheduled Tribes (Adivasis), women, as well as ideological and religious minorities, as a recent Amnesty International report[18] has highlighted. Equally worrying, rapes are being increasingly used as an instrument to intimidate and silence,[19] as evidenced in the gang rape and murder of eight-year-old Asifa Bano, who was targeted simply because right-wing groups wanted her Muslim community to leave the area.[20] Possibly deriving legitimacy from one of their ideologues,[21] legislators and right-wing groups affiliated to the ruling party have even intervened on behalf of the perpetrators.[22] Violence has become the first and last response to any situation that does not conform to the norms to which these private militias prescribe to. However, there seemingly appears to be a method to the madness. After all, it was the Manusmriti's exhortation that 'punishment alone governs all beings . . . The whole world is kept in order by punishment'.[23] It wouldn't be too far-fetched to argue that some of these private militias (and their political benefactors) are methodically using violence to establish new social and political authority.

In most of these, the state has been partisan in the application of the rule of law,[24] which increasingly seems to be contingent on conformity to the ruling party's ideology. It has either delayed arresting perpetrators, such as the legislator who allegedly raped a girl in Unnao, Uttar Pradesh,[25] or clamped down on demonstrators, like in Mandsaur, Madhya Pradesh, where the police opened fire without warning on farmers demanding fair prices for their crops[26] or arrested journalists[27] who have dared to report on uncomfortable facts.

This escalating spiral of violence not only destabilizes the country, but also delegitimizes the sovereignty of the state, which no longer enjoys a monopoly on force. This abdication of sovereign functions has created a pervasive distrust of not just the ruling party but also state institutions. Far from being seen as the penultimate moral authority, today the state is viewed as just another contending stakeholder, untethered from both constitutional and institutional values.

Diverse social groups, whether Dalits, farmers, Adivasis, students, minorities or dominant castes, are increasingly relying on their own agency to organize their lives and claim their rights. This also includes some Opposition-governed states, which are suggesting coalitions such as the Dravidian Cooperation to counter the state's studied indifference towards them.[28] There is a pervasive fear that the state is no longer a wide arena of interaction between contrarian interests, and is unwilling to mediate conflicts over access to opportunities and resources. This severely compromises the larger unity of the nation-state.

What Young Indians Believe

And yet, we cannot deny that this chaos may have been seen as disruptive, and even necessary, by large sections of society. Authoritarianism in India doesn't just feed on the anger at the social and cultural elite (which has been caricatured as the 'Lutyens/Khan Market Gang'[29]), but is a product of that anger. This authoritarianism not only acknowledges but deliberately exacerbates the fact that India's youth is deeply conservative (socially), very religious and driven by caste norms, as a 2017 Centre for the Study of Developing Societies (CSDS) and Konrad Adenauer Stiftung (KAS) study[30] highlighted. It understands that even though India is divided by caste, religion, language, gender and aspirations, it is angry at being *left out* (because of poor access to English education, to opportunities of employment, to power, and most of all, to the kind of life they see in popular culture and everyday life) and even angrier at being *held behind* (because of nepotism, corruption and supposedly unfair state patronage towards minorities and historically marginalized communities). Shockingly, they also fear that civil society organizations, non-governmental organizations, the intelligentsia and sections of the media are instruments of the elite deployed to maintain the status quo. Even though some of these notions are fuelled by atavistic prejudices that have no place in a civilized society, the bitter reality is that many Indians hold this elite responsible for their plight.

Young and impatient, Indians yearn for *samman* (respect and dignity), *samruddhi* (progress and prosperity) and, most of all, vikas (development). These mean different things to different people. For example, to a non-dominant Dalit or OBC sub-caste, vikas is entwined with samman, and means both economic *and* social mobility, since the dominant sub-caste has received the lion's share of benefits and acquired cultural capital. To a dominant community (the Marathas in Maharashtra, Jats in Haryana, Reddys and Kapus in Andhra Pradesh and Telangana, Gujjars in Rajasthan, etc.), vikas means access to opportunities that stem from educational qualifications (samruddhi), which has become especially urgent given that land has gradually stopped being a guaranteed source of economic and social well-being. Similarly, vikas in a village means a road and cheap public transport since they represent opportunity. In a metro, a road represents a non-negotiable public good. To a woman in a village, vikas represents the safety of a four-walled toilet, which shields her from harassment and gives her a sense of agency. Most of all, vikas–samruddhi–samman to the youth mean a muscular, aggressive India that demands respect from the world.

This last phenomenon is something that is seldom acknowledged or appreciated. Anecdotally, a significant portion of India's youth feels that India is a great civilization that has not got its due from the world. They increasingly feel and demand that the state protect and enhance national, community and individual pride, which are intermeshed like never before. In fact, it may not be too far off the mark to assume that it is also felt that it is the citizen's primordial identity (racial, religious, political, linguistic, etc.) that should be the basis for a claim on the goods and services that the state is mandated to provide.

Without a doubt, we are at the front lines in a battle for India's soul. This battle is also one for the world order. The epistemic convulsions that India is undergoing today mirrors global trends. Austria, Australia, Brazil, Italy, Spain, the USA and numerous other countries have all been subject to similar pressures. The machismo politicians, authoritarianism, xenophobia, attacks on the establishment, and the frenzied efforts to restore the nation-state to a golden period are all symptoms of a larger structural malaise. Apart from environmental upheavals and mass migrations, the unchecked flow of capital across borders (which has considerably weakened the nation-state's control over taxation and hence the resources available for national development) has created large-scale inequities and loss of agency. The resultant frustrations at the state's inability to meet its socio-economic commitments are being cynically redirected by right-wing parties at 'enemies' (internal and external), deflected by pointless military exploits, and assuaged by massive public relations exercises. Clearly, the existential threat to the nation-state is a by-product of the pandemic threat to the world order.

Our response to this systemic crisis would perforce have to be twofold—transnational and national. At the transnational level, like-minded think tanks, movements, and political parties should strive to coordinate strategies and share ideas on how to jointly create a more liberal, secular and progressive world order. In striving to forge consensus on key issues, they should foremost reimagine global governance, including creating a new transnational political mechanism. This mechanism would perforce need to supervise cross-border money flows and reimagine the whole gamut of financial regulation. Without doing this urgently, the nation-state will simply not have the financial or technological resources to deliver on its welfare commitments. Similarly, there needs to be a coordinated approach to combating the fallouts of climate change, as well as economic inequities. Addressing these can very substantially temper the legitimate tensions caused by a stagnant and declining quality of life.

At the national level, it is high time liberal-, secular- and republican-minded citizens committed to safeguarding the constitutional idea of India (henceforth progressive forces) stop focusing our energies on vanquishing the 'other', which not only separates and antagonizes, but also creates further chaos. It might be infinitely more meaningful if we were to understand why ordinary Indians have strayed from the dream that our founders had dreamt. Without doing that, how can we win back the hearts and minds of our fellow Indians? If we cannot even discuss, let alone agree on, who and where we are, then how are we to move forward as a society? If India is to rise to ever greater heights and take her rightful place in the fellowship of nations, it is imperative that we listen to each other and accommodate different dreams to become more than our individual parts. Now, more than ever, we need to work *together* to establish the foundations of a new India for a new time.

Uniting Progressive Forces

The battles of the last five years have brought together like-minded progressive forces in a tenuous and fragile alliance. Even though they are united in their earnestness to safeguard constitutional values, they have been suspicious of each other's motives, and jealously guard crumbling territories. Transactional and instrumental, this alliance has been found wanting, as the experience of the 2019 Lok Sabha elections proved. And post the election, they have all but withdrawn into old animosities and now either seek to primarily secure their individual interests or are too despondent to raise their voices. This simply cannot do. We need to forge principled alliances and institutionalize functional networks that can defend India's constitutional principles. This is a fateful moment for us all, and history will judge us for what we do next. As Martin Luther King, Jr, once said, 'Those of us who love peace must organize as effectively as the war hawks.'[31]

All those in India who count themselves progressives, as this author unequivocally does, need to understand that we are stronger together, and because of each other. We will have to carefully listen to our fellow Indians, and not just hear what we want to hear. And most of all, we will have to be compassionate in our policies and constructive in our politics.

Indians are thirsty for leadership that understands them and addresses their individual needs and aspirations. We will simply have to re-articulate our visions for India in a manner which appeals to different sections of society. We need to learn that exhortations to protect the Constitution or the nation, which are extremely important, do not enthuse people with extremely individualistic aspirations. We will have to weave their multiple stories into a national one, and wield them to counter those that seek to impose a unitary story on India. As Salman Rushdie's *Haroun and the Sea of Stories* tells us, the land of *gup* (stories) always wins over the land of *chup* (silence).

We will also need to radically reinvent our political strategies and operational methodologies. To do this successfully, we will have to move beyond the 'spectacle politics' that we have all got used to. Dharnas, petitions, legislative obstruction and high-decibel mobilizations on the media (social, electronic and print) may ensure accountability, but they cannot organically move people to associate with a party or leader or cause. These can only temporarily enthral. We will therefore have to methodically form relationships with individuals in each household. As others have done successfully, we need to leverage all mediums (personal interactions, social media forums and messaging services, popular culture, etc.) to constantly engage in a dialogue on things that matter to the people. Unless we do so tactically, at every panchayat and municipality in every election hence, we will not be a beacon of hope in the gathering darkness.

To do this, we need to begin by rethinking current social, political and economic paradigms. Unless we evolve a framework to rediscover India, we cannot be responsive to the needs, aspirations and dreams of our fellow Indians. Without doing that, we cannot establish 'more co-operative, anti-hierarchical forms of socio-economic and political organization, as envisaged by MK Gandhi'.[32] In striving to kickstart a national dialogue on key socio-economic and political issues, this ambitious set of volumes aims to do just that. It hopes to create a symphony from the multiple voices of India, and thereby forge a consensus on how we can proceed as a society.

Ultimately, the battles of the last five years and those of the next five years are a clarion call for all of us who have been inevitably committed to furthering India's promise. As India's first prime minister, Jawaharlal Nehru, once said, 'The future is not one of ease or resting but of incessant striving so that we may fulfil the pledges we have so often taken and the one we shall take today. The service of India means the service of the millions who suffer. It means the ending of poverty and ignorance and disease and inequality of opportunity . . . And so we have to labour and to work, and work hard, to give reality to our dreams. Those dreams are for India, but they are also for the world.'[33]

Notes

Introduction

1. Bharat Karnad, *Why India Is Not a Great Power (Yet)* (New Delhi: Oxford University Press, 2015), p. 1.
2. B.R. Ambedkar, *Waiting for a Visa*, in *Dr Babasaheb Ambedkar Writings and Speeches, Vol. 12*, ed. Vasant Moon (Mumbai: Education Department, Government of Maharashtra, 1993).
3. Rohan Venkataramakrishnan, 'The Daily Fix: What Does Rohith Vemula's Suicide Mean to Us Today?', Scroll, https://scroll.in/article/826910/the-daily-fix-what-does-rohith-vemulas-suicide-mean-to-us-today
4. Ashwarya K.S., 'Dr Payal Tadvi: the Reservation and the Violence it Evokes', Round Table India, https://www.roundtableindia.co.in/~roundta3/index.php?option=com_content&view=article&id=9653:a-note-on-caste-violence-in-colleges&catid=129:events-and-activism&Itemid=195
5. Deen Dayal Upadhyaya, *Integral Humanism: An Analysis of Some Basic Elements* (New Delhi: Prabhat Prakashan, 2016), p. 101.
6. Benedict Anderson, *Imagined Communities: Reflections on the Origin and Spread of Nationalism* (London: Verso, 1983), p. 49.

7. Jawaharlal Nehru, *The Discovery of India* (New Delhi: Penguin India, 2008).
8. V.D. Savarkar, *Hindutva: Who Is a Hindu* (Bombay: Hindi Sahitya Sadan, 1988).
9. M.S. Golwalkar, *We or Our Nationhood Defined* (Nagpur: Bharat Prakashan, 1944).
10. Antiphon, 'On Truth', *Oxyrhynchus Papyri* XI, no. 1364, fragment 1.

Epic, Narrative and Lyric Ideas of India

1. https://www.geolsoc.org.uk
2. W.J. Bate, *Negative Capability: The Intuitive Approach in Keats*. Introduction by Maura Del Serra (New York: Contra Mundum Press, 2012).
3. https://www.jaina.org/page/11_17_16_Newsletter/JAINA-Newsletter-Aparigraha-Know-your-Tirthankar-Jain-Center-News.htm
4. G.N. Devy, 'Love Is a Battlefield', *Telegraph*, 3 May 2019, http://indianquarterly.com/love-is-a-battlefield
5. 'Annihilation of Caste' is an undelivered speech written in 1936 by B.R. Ambedkar who fought against the country's practice of untouchability. It was later self-published by the author, originally in 15 May 1936. It was reprinted by Navayana with an Introduction by Arundhati Roy in 2015.
6. G.N. Devy, 'Our Routinely Truncated Definitions of Citizenship', *Telegraph*, 4 January 2019, https://www.telegraphindia.com/opinion/our-routinely-truncated-definitions-of-citizenship/cid/1680747
7. William Sleeman, *Rambles and Recollections of an Indian Officer* (London: J. Hatchard, 1844); G.N. Devy, *A Nomad Called Thief* (Orient Blackswan, 2007).
8. Report of the special task group appointed by the Government of India for denotified and nomadic tribes, and chaired by the author of this essay, 2008.
9. G.N. Devy, 'The Post-Truth Era Is Ironically Making Gandhi More Relevant', *Telegraph*, 7 December 2018, https://www.

telegraphindia.com/opinion/the-post-truth-era-is-ironically-making-gandhi-more relevant/cid/1677855

10. G.N. Devy, 'Breaking of Vidyasagar Statue Shows That Intolerance towards Diverse Ideas and Dissent Has Taken Hold of Our Minds', *Telegraph*, 6 June 2019, https://www.telegraphindia.com/opinion/breaking-of-vidyasagar-statue-shows-that-intolerance-towards-diverse-ideas-and-dissent-has-taken-hold-of-our-minds/cid/1691849

11. Adolf Hitler, *Mein Kampf* (Bombay: Jaico, 1988), p. 48.

12. G.N. Devy, 'When Questions Erupt', *Telegraph*, 2 August 2018, https://www.telegraphindia.com/opinion/when-questions-erupt/cid/1467814

13. Una and Unnao are names of places associated with heinous atrocities involving mob-lynching and rape.

A Land of Belonging

1. Versions of this essay have previously appeared in 'The Idea of an Ever-Ever Land', Nidhi Razdan, *Left, Right and Centre* (New Delhi: Penguin Random House India, 2017); Shashi Tharoor, *India: From Midnight to the Millennium* (New Delhi: Penguin India, 1997); Tharoor, *The Paradoxical Prime Minister* (New Delhi: Aleph Book Company, 2018); Tharoor, *An Era of Darkness: The British Empire in India* (New Delhi: Aleph Book Company, 2016).

2. Jawaharlal Nehru, *A Tryst with Destiny*, Nehru Memorial Museum and Library, http://nehrumemorial.nic.in/en/gift-gallery.html?id=214&tmpl=component

3. Richard Langworth, *Churchill: In His Own Words* (London: Ebury Press, 2012), p. 163.

4. Shashi Tharoor, 'E Pluribus, India: Is Indian Modernity Working?' *Foreign Affairs* 77.1 (1998): 128–134.

5. Mughal emperor Jehangir, while visiting Kashmir in the seventeenth century.

6. Edward A. Gargan, 'A Revolution Transforms India: Socialism's Out, Free Market In', *New York Times*, 29 March 1992,

https://www.nytimes.com/1992/03/29/world/a-revolution-transforms-india-socialism-s-out-free-market-in.html

7. Pankaj Mishra, 'In Defence of Reason', *Guardian*, 9 July 2005.
8. Shashi Tharoor, *An Era of Darkness: The British Empire in India* (New Delhi: Aleph Book Company, 2016).
9. Diana Eck, *India: A Sacred Geography* (New York: Harmony, 2013).
10. Massimo Taparelli d'Azeglio, 'Italy in Translation', Free Library, https://www.thefreelibrary.com/Translator%27s+introduction%3A+%22Italy+in+translation%22-a0159536327
11. Shashi Tharoor, *Riot: A Love Story* (New Delhi: Penguin Books India, 2003).

Secularism: Central to a Democratic Nation

1. Mark Anthony in *The Tragedy of Julius Caesar* (3.2.216–19) from Stanley Wells and Gary Taylor, eds, *The Oxford Shakespeare* (Oxford: Oxford University Press, 1994).
2. News18, 'Lok Sabha Election Results: In Victory Speech, Narendra Modi Likens 2019 Polls to Mahabharata, Says Will Take Rivals along Too', 23 May 2019, https://www.news18.com/news/politics/lok-sabha-election-results-in-victory-speech-narendra-modi-likens-2019-polls-to-mahabharata-says-will-take-rivals-along-too-2157207.html
3. *The Communal Problem: Report of the Committee Appointed by the Indian National Congress (Karachi Session 1931) to Enquire into the Kanpur Riot of March 1931* (Delhi: National Book Trust, 2005).
4. *The Collected Works of Mahatma Gandhi, Vol. 45* (New Delhi: Publications Division, Ministry of Information and Broadcasting, 1971), p. 372.
5. 'Constitutional Provisions of the Sapru Committee 1945', cited in Neera Chandhoke, *Beyond Secularism, The Rights of Religious Minorities* (Delhi: Oxford University Press, 1999), pp. 59, 76.
6. S. Gopal, 'Nehru and Minorities', *Economic and Political Weekly* 23 (Special Issue), 45–47 (November 1988): 2463–65 and 2466.

7. *Constituent Assembly Debates, Vol. 10* (New Delhi: Lok Sabha Secretariat, 1989), pp. 439, 444, 446.
8. Ibid, p. 441.
9. Jawaharlal Nehru, 'A Common Cultural Inheritance', in *Selected Works of Jawaharlal Nehru , Vol. 5* (New Delhi: Oxford University Press, 1987), p. 26.
10. Jawaharlal Nehru, 'A Secular State', in *Jawaharlal Nehru: An Anthology*, ed. S. Gopal (New Delhi: Oxford University Press, 1980), p. 330.
11. Dhananjay Mahapatra, 'Secularism Not Aloofness to Religion: SC', *Times of India*, 28 October 2016, https://timesofindia.indiatimes.com/india/Secularism-not-aloofness-to-religion-SC/articleshow/55102751.cms
12. Gary Jacobsohn, *The Wheel of Law: India's Secularism in Comparative Constitutional Context* (New Delhi: Oxford University Press, 2003), pp. 145–215.
13. Jawaharlal Nehru, *The Discovery of India* (Delhi: Penguin, 1946), p. 33.

Indian Nationalism versus Hindutva Nationalism

1. Lara Seligman and Robbie Gramer, 'Amid Re-Election Campaign, Modi Takes the Fight to Pakistan', *Foreign Policy*, 27 February 2019.
2. Una Galani, 'India Insight: Money Power Is Choking Democracy', *Reuters*, 4 March 2019.
3. Wire, 'In 2019, Is BJP Riding a Modi Wave or a Money Wave?' 6 May 2019.
4. Siddharth Bhatia, 'The Reputation of the Election Commission Has Been Severely Tarnished', Wire, 20 May 2019.
5. Firstpost, 'Modi Talks "Nationalism", BJP Explains "Freedom of Speech" at Party's National Level Pre-Poll Huddle', 20 March 2016.
6. See the government's own press release, https://pib.gov.in/newsite/PrintRelease.aspx?relid=191728
7. Akeel Bilgrami, 'Introduction', *Social Scientist* 39.1/2 (January–February 2011): 1–2.

8. V.D. Savarkar, *Hindutva: Who Is a Hindu?* (Delhi: Bharati Sahitya Sadan, 1989).

9. Akeel Bilgrami, 'Introduction', *Social Scientist* 39.1/2 (January–February 2011): 2.

10. Ibid.

11. M.S. Golwalkar, *We or Our Nationhood Defined* (Nagpur: Bharat Publications, 1939), p. 6.

12. Ibid, pp. 43–44.

13. Jawaharlal Nehru, *The Discovery of India* (New York: John Day, 1946), p. 59

14. Rabindranath Tagore, 'A Hymn to India', *Indian Literature* 1.2 (April–September 1958), p. 1.

15. See, for example, ICF Team, 'Re-writing History, Saffronising Education: Remembering Nangeli Lest Government Makes Us Forget', NewsClick, 19 March 2019; and, Sanjay Jha, 'Saffronisation of a Nation', *Pioneer*, 28 May 2019.

16. George Lukács, *The Destruction of Reason* (London: Merlin, 1980).

17. Reported and cited in https://www.bbc.com/news/uk-37995600

18. Even as mainstream outlets like *India Today* routinely report on the regimes of violence unleashed by groups like the gau rakshaks; see, 'Muslim Couple Thrashed by Gau Rakshaks, Made to Shout Jai Shree Ram, 5 Arrested', *India Today*, 25 May 2019.

19. Wire, 'When Sardar Patel Took on the "Forces of Hate" and Banned the RSS', Wire, 31 October 2018.

20. Wire, 'In 2019, Is BJP Riding a Modi Wave or a Money Wave?' 6 May 2019.

21. Among numerous instances, see NewsClick, '15 Arrested for Sedition for Celebrating Pakistan's Cricket Victory', 21 June 2017; and *Pioneer*, 'BJP Misused Sedition Law to Jail Political Rivals: Punia', 5 April 2019.

22. Wire, 'Sedition Law Must Not be Invoked for Critical Social Media Posts: Chhattisgarh CM Baghel', 16 June 2019.

23. For evidence, see https://www.indiatoday.in/news-analysis/story/are-naxals-amit-shah-s-next-target-1592135-2019-08-27

From the Largest Democracy to the Greatest Democracy

1. http://worldpopulationreview.com/countries/india-population
2. Caleb Silver, 'Top 20 Economies in the World', Investopedia, 7 June 2019, https://www.investopedia.com/insights/worlds top economies/#6-india-gdp
3. https://archive.india.gov.in/overseas/diaspora/nri.php; https:// en.wikipedia.org/wiki/Non-resident_Indian_and_person_of_ Indian_origin (accessed 9 June 2019).
4. https://www.livemint.com/news/india/india-tops-remittances-list-received-79-billion-in-2018-1554779601589.html
5. Press Trust of India, 'India's Richest 1% Corner 73% of Wealth Generation: Survey', *Times of India*, 22 January 2018, https://timesofindia.indiatimes.com/business/india-business/ indias-richest-1-corner-73-of-wealth-generation-survey/ articleshow/62598222.cms
6. Joanna Slater, 'India Is No Longer Home to the Largest Number of Poor People in the World. Nigeria Is', *Washington Post*, 10 July 2018, https://www.washingtonpost.com/news/ worldviews/wp/2018/07/10/india-is-no-longer-home-to-the-largest-number-of-poor-people-in-the-world-nigeria-is/?noredirect=on&utm_term=.021a44ab3587
7. https://economictimes.indiatimes.com/news/politics-and-nation/india-has-one-third-of-worlds-stunted-children-global-nutrition-report/articleshow/66865016.cms
8. *India Today,* 'India Home to 46.6 Million Stunted Children, a Third of World's Total: Global Nutrition Report 2018', 30 November 2018, https://www.indiatoday.in/education-today/gk-current-affairs/story/india-home-to-46-6-million-stunted-children-a-third-of-world-s-total-global-nutrition-report-2018-1399576-2018-11-30
9. Jitendra, 'Human Development Index: India Climbs One Spot to 130', *Down To Earth*, 15 September 2018, https://www. downtoearth.org.in/news/economy/human-development-index-india-climbs-one-spot-to-130-61631
10. Richard Mahapatra, 'World's Working-Age Population Growing Slowest in Over 2 Decades', *Down to Earth*, 16 February 2019, https://

www.downtoearth.org.in/news/economy/world-s-working-age-population-growing-slowest-in-over-2-decades-63263

11. Ayaka Miyazawa, 'Be Astonished by Japanese Population Pyramid', *YC News*, 1 November 2018, http://www.theycnews.com/2018/11/01/be-astonished-by-japanese-population-pyramid; http://www.newindianexpress.com/world/2018/sep/17/over-28-per-cent-of-japanese-population-officially-old-government-1873096.html; https://www.mckinsey.com/featured-insights/asia-pacific/japan-lessons-from-a-hyperaging-society; https://economictimes.indiatimes.com/news/economy/indicators/indias-gdp-will-be-bigger-than-japan-germany-combined-in-4-years-imf/articleshow/46585441.cms?from=mdr

12. https://www.economicshelp.org/blog/8950/society/impact-ageing-population-economy

13. Tom Phillips, 'China Ends One-Child Policy After 35 Years', *Guardian*, 29 October 2015, https://www.theguardian.com/world/2015/oct/29/china-abandons-one-child-policy

14. Gyan Varma and Elizabeth Roche, 'PM-Elect Narendra Modi to Take Oath on 30 May', *Livemint*, 26 May 2019, https://www.livemint.com/elections/lok-sabha-elections/narendra-modi-to-be-sworn-in-as-prime-minister-on-may-30-1558872290858.html

15. *Economic Times*, '50% India's Working-Age Population Out of Labour Force, Says Report', 4 February 2019, https://economictimes.indiatimes.com/jobs/50-indias-working-age-population-out-of-labour-force-says-report/articleshow/67830482.cms?from=mdr

16. *Business Today*, 'India's Unemployment Rate Hit Four-Decade High of 6.1% in 2017–18, Says NSSO Survey', 31 January 2019, https://www.businesstoday.in/current/economy-politics/india-unemployment-rate-hits-four-decade-high-of-6-pct-in-2017-says-nsso-survey/story/315420.html

17. Press Trust of India, 'Over 80 per cent Engineering Graduates in India Unemployable: Study', *Economic Times*, 24 January 2016, https://economictimes.indiatimes.com/jobs/over-80-per-cent-engineering-graduates-in-india-unemployable-study/articleshow/50703662.cms?from=mdr

18. Venkatesh Ganesh, Tina Edwin, Jinoy Jose P. and A. Srinivas, 'We Don't Need This Education', *The Hindu BusinessLine*, 18 June 2018, https://www.thehindubusinessline.com/specials/india-file/semi-urban-and-rural-india-grapples-with-skillset-problems-rendering-youth-unemployable/article24194788.ece

19. S.Y. Quraishi, '67 Years Young', *Indian Express*, 18 August 2014, https://indianexpress.com/article/opinion/columns/67-years-young

20. https://www.prsindia.org/report-summaries/draft-national-education-policy-2019

21. http://worldpopulationreview.com/countries/india-population

22. *The Hindu BusinessLine*, 'In Just 8 years, India Will Overtake China as World's Most Populous Country: UN Report', *The Hindu BusinessLine*, 17 June 2019, https://www.thehindubusinessline.com/economy/india-will-overtake-china-as-worlds-most-populous-country-in-2027-un-report/article28021947.ece

23. https://mhrd.gov.in/sites/upload_files/mhrd/files/statistics/ESG2016_0.pdf; *Report of the Working Group on Adolescents for the Tenth Five Year Plan* (New Delhi: Planning Commission, Government of India, 2001), p. 8, http://www.planningcommission.nic.in/aboutus/committee/wrkgrp/wg_adolcnts.pdf

24. https://www.quotes.net/quote/67261

25. https://economictimes.indiatimes.com/news/politics-and-nation/kathua-rape-case-verdict/articleshow/69720996.cms?from=mdr; https://www.ndtv.com/india-news/unnao-girl-alleges-no-action-on-gang-rape-sets-herself-afire-with-mother-2092492

26. Dipankar De Sarkar, 'Crimes against Women Going Unpunished', *Livemint*, 18 October 2018, https://www.livemint.com/Opinion/082sNzCGFJwaCKuigUKYKK/Opinion--Crimes-against-women-going-unpunished.html

27. Press Trust of India, 'Female Labour Force Participation in India Fell to 26% in 2018: Report', *The Hindu*, 8 March 2019, https://www.thehindu.com/business/female-labour-force-participation-in-india-fell-to-26-in-2018-report/article26467857.ece

28. Tish Sanghera, 'Rural Unemployment: When Jobs Disappear, Women Are the First to Lose Out', *Business Standard*, 17 April

2019, https://www.business-standard.com/article/economy-policy/rural-unemployment-when-jobs-disappear-women-are-the-first-to-lose-out-119041700134_1.html

29. https://www.livemint.com/Politics/TOZ8tlmWzw HfXeJ3ffyQMM/Womens-ownership-of-land-in-rural-areas-can-help-cut-povert.html

30. Press Trust of India, 'India Ranks 95 among 129 Countries in Global Gender Equality Index', *YourStory*, 5 June 2019, https://yourstory.com/socialstory/2019/06/india-ranks-95-global-gender-equality-index

31. http://hdr.undp.org/en/content/gender-development-index-gdi; https://en.wikipedia.org/wiki/Gender_Development_Index

32. Press Trust of India, '60% of People Defecating in the Open in World Live in India: WHO report', *Hindustan Times*, 4 August 2014, https://www.hindustantimes.com/india/60-of-people-defecating-in-the-open-in-world-live-in-india-who-report/story-gHdORFHYsmJycRQkjyuiJM.html

33. Neetu Chandra Sharma, 'Swachh Bharat Mission Improved Health and Nutrition: Economic Survey', *Livemint*, 4 July 2019, https://www.livemint.com/budget/economic-survey/swachh-bharat-mission-improved-health-and-nutrition-economic-survey-1562238271723.html

34. Rupali Pruthi, 'Swachh Bharat Mission (G): Over 96 percent of Households in Rural India Actually Use Toilets', Jagran Josh, 5 March 2019, https://www.jagranjosh.com/current-affairs/swachh-bharat-mission-g-over-96-percent-of-households-in-rural-india-actually-use-toilets-1551789154-1

35. Chandra Sharma, 'Swachh Bharat Mission improved health and nutrition: Economic Survey', *Livemint*, 4 July 2019.

36. NewsClick, 'Corporate Media is a Hate Mongering Factory', 1 March 2019, https://www.newsclick.in/corporate-media-hate-mongering-factory

37. Scroll, 'Rising Hate Crimes and Intolerance Can Seriously Damage Economy, Warns Industrialist Adi Godrej', 13 July 2019,

https://scroll.in/latest/930423/rising-hate-crimes-and-intolerance-can-seriously-damage-economy-warns industrialist adi-godrej

38. Subodh Varma, 'Jharkhand's 14th Lynching in Four Years, Country's 266th', NewsClick, 25 June 2019, https://www.newsclick.in/Mob-Lynching-India-Jharkhand-Hate-Crimes

39. https://www.counterpunch.org/2002/08/06/fit-for-democracy-vs-fit-through-democracy

40. S.Y. Quraishi, 'A Welcome Debate on Electoral Reforms', *The Hindu*, 12 July 2019, https://www.thehindu.com/opinion/lead/a-welcome-debate-on-electoral-reforms/article28391880.ece

41. *Business Standard,* '"Weak-kneed": 66 Ex-bureaucrats Write to President Kovind on EC's Conduct', 9 April 2019, https://www.business-standard.com/article/elections/misuse-of-electoral-process-by-ec-and-bjp-write-66-ex-bureaucrats-to-prez-119040900239_1.html

42. S.Y. Quraishi, 'It's Time to Take Stock of the Electoral Process', *The Hindu*, 24 May 2019, https://www.thehindu.com/opinion/op-ed/its-time-to-take-stock-of-the-electoral-process/article27239174.ece

A Shared Past, an Uncertain Future

1. The Khwaja Altaf Husain Hali poems are from rare manuscripts in a private family collection. The translations are my own.

2. Allama Mohammad Iqbal, *Kulliyat-e-Iqbal* (Lahore: Ferozsons, 1950), p. 88. My own translation.

3. Ibid, p. 89.

4. Ibid, p. 90.

5. Ibid, p. 177.

6. Ibid, p. 178.

7. Ibid, p. 179.

8. Available at https://urdushahkar.org/parda-kushaaii-na-ho-saki-tilok-chand-mahroom. My own translation.

9. The Khwaja Altaf Husain Hali poems are from rare manuscripts in a private family collection. The translations are my own.

10. Ibid.
11. https://www.independent.co.uk/news/world/asia/india-muslim-man-lynch-mob-killed-tabrez-ansari-video-jharkand-a8971611.html
12. *India's Maulana Abul Kalam Azad*, *Vol. 4*, ed. Syeda Saiyidain Hameed (New Delhi: ICCR and Vikas Publishing, 1990).
13. https://www.hindustantimes.com/cities/jharkhand-man-beaten-by-mob-forced-to-chant-jai-sri-ram-dies/story-S0AgXAgihEMMrPuamm3GtJ.html
14. *India's Maulana Abul Kalam Azad*, *Vol. 4*, ed. Syeda Saiyidain Hameed.
15. The poem by Raghupati Sahay, aka Firaq Gorakhpuri, is from a rare manuscript in a private family collection. The translations are my own.

The Fate of Shudras in a Buffalo Nation

1. Kancha Ilaiah Shepherd, *Buffalo Nationalism, A Critique of Spiritual Fascism* (New Delhi: Sage India, 2019).
2. Kancha Ilaiah Shepherd, *Why I Am Not a Hindu: A Sudra Critique of Hindutva Philosophy, Culture and Political Economy* (New Delhi: Sage India, 2019).
3. Ibid.
4. M.S. Golwalkar, *We or Our Nationhood Defined* (Nagpur: Bharat Prakashan, 1939), pp. 54–55.
5. Press Trust of India, 'RSS Chief for Relook at Quota Policy', *The Hindu*, 21 September 2015, https://www.thehindu.com/news/national/other-states/rss-chief-mohan-bhagwat-for-relook-at-quota-policy/article7671684.ece
6. Kancha Ilaiah Shepherd, 'The BJP–RSS, 10 Percent EWS Reservation, and the Unreserved Shudras', Citizen, https://www.thecitizen.in/index.php/en/NewsDetail/index/4/16285/The-BJP-RSS-10-Percent-EWS-Reservation-and-the-Unreserved-Shudras
7. Golwalkar, *We or Our Nationhood Defined*.
8. Ibid.

9.   Wendy Doniger, *The Laws of Manu* (New Delhi: Penguin India, 2000).

10. Kancha Ilaiah Shepherd, 'Hinduism Denies Spiritual Citizenship and "Moksha" to Shudras, Dalits and Adivasis', News18, https://www.news18.com/news/opinion/opinion-hinduism-denies-spiritual-citizenship-to-shudras-dalits-and-adivasis-1949743.html

11. Kancha Ilaiah Shepherd, 'Where Are the Shudras?', *Caravan*, October 2018, https://caravanmagazine.in/caste/why-the-shudras-are-lost-in-today-india

12. Mysore Narasimhachar Srinivas, 'The Dominant Caste in Rampura', *American Anthropologist* 61.1 (1959): 1–16.

13. Harbans Mukhia, 'Was There Feudalism in Indian History?', *Journal of Peasant Studies* 8.3 (1 April 1981): 273–310, https://doi.org/10.1080/03066158108438139

14. Aakar Patel, 'Make a Dalit or Adivasi Woman the RSS Chief', *National Herald*, 8 April 2018, https://www.nationalheraldindia.com/opinion/aakar-patel-bjp-should-ask-rss-to-appoint-a-dalit-or-adivasi-woman-as-its-chief

15. Bhimrao Ramji Ambedkar, 'Who Were the Shudras?', in *Dr Babasaheb Ambedkar Writings & Speeches, Vol. 7* (Bombay: Government of Maharastra, 1990), pp. 42–56.

16. Shrutisagar Yamunan, 'Not against Non-Brahmins Becoming Priests, Says RSS State President', *The Hindu*, 2015, https://www.thehindu.com/news/cities/chennai/not-against-nonbrahmins-becoming-priests-says-rss-state-president/article7839676.ece.

17. O.B. Roopesh, 'When "Anybody Can Be Brahmin"', *Economic and Political Weekly* 52.46 (November 2017), https://www.epw.in/journal/2017/46/commentary/when-'anybody-can-be-brahmin'.html

18. Mahatma Jotirao Phule, *Slavery* (Bombay: Education Department, Government of Maharashtra, 1991), p. 91.

19. Robert Pryor, 'Bodh Gaya in the 1950s: Jawaharlal Nehru, Mahant Giri and Anagarika Munindrao', in *Cross-Disciplinary Perspectives on a Contested Buddhist Site: Bodh Gaya Jataka*, eds. Abishek Geary, David, Sayers, Matthew R. and Singh Amar (London: Routledge, 2012), pp. 112–13.

20. Ajaz Ashraf, 'A Short Account of India's Long History of Hypocrisy on Cow Slaughter Laws', *Dawn*, 2 October 2015, https://www.dawn.com/news/1210215/a-short-account-of-indias-long-history-of-hypocrisy-on-cow-slaughter-laws

21. Aakar Patel, '10 Reasons Why Leonardo DiCaprio Shouldn't Preach Vegetarianism to Indians', *Economic Times*, 3 July 2016, https://economictimes.indiatimes.com/magazines/panache/10-reasons-why-leonardo-dicaprio-shouldnt-preach-vegetarianism-to-indians/articleshow/53030029.cms?from=mdr

22. Mahatma Gandhi, *Autobiography: The Story of My Experiments with Truth* (Courier Corporation, 1983); Jawaharlal Nehru, *Toward Freedom: The Autobiography of Jawaharlal Nehru* (John Day Co, 1942).

23. D. Ajit, 'Corporate Boards in India', *Economic and Political Weekly* 47.32 (August 2012), https://www.epw.in/journal/2012/32/insight/corporate-boards-india.html

24. *Times of India*, 'Union Cabinet 2019: PM Tries to Accommodate Most Castes', 2019, https://timesofindia.indiatimes.com/india/union-cabinet-2019-pm-tries-to-accommodate-most-castes/articleshow/69589639.cms.

25. D. Ajit, 'Corporate Boards in India', *Economic and Political Weekly*.

26. Kuffir, 'The Bahujan Have a Common Enemy', Round Table India, 2019, https://roundtableindia.co.in/index.php?option=com_content&view=article&id=9634:how-constitutional-is-10-ews-economically-weaker-sections-reservation&catid=119:feature&Itemid=132

27. M.S.S. Pandian, *Brahmin & Non-Brahmin, Genealogies of the Tamil Political Present* (New Delhi: Permanent Black, 2017), pp. 77–84.

28. Kancha Ilaiah Shepherd, 'RSS/BJP and the Shudra Neo-Slaves', Countercurrents.org, 2018, https://countercurrents.org/2018/11/rss-bjp-and-the-shudra-neo-slaves

29. Patel, 'Make a Dalit or Adivasi Woman the RSS Chief', *National Herald*.

30. Aakar Patel, 'The Peculiar Pedigree of the Business Class', *Livemint*, 2011, https://www.livemint.com/Leisure/LIA5OcknCv3zQw2hJi0GDN/The-peculiar-pedigree-of-the-business-class.html

31. Praveena Kodoth, 'Courting Legitimacy or Delegitimizing Custom? Sexuality, Sambandham, and Marriage Reform in Late Nineteenth-Century Malabar', *Modern Asian Studies* 35.2 (2001): 349–84, http://www.jstor.org/stable/313121

32. *New Indian Express*, 'Kerala Nair Service Society Voices Strong Opposition to Women Entering Sabarimala', 26 July 2019, http://www.newindianexpress.com/specials/2018/jul/26/kerala-nair-service-society-voices-strong-opposition-to-women-entering-sabarimala-1848673.html

33. The full text of the Supreme Court judgement can be accessed at https://barandbench.com/wp-content/uploads/2018/09/Sabarimala-Indu-Malhotra-J-judgment.pdf

34. Aneesha Mathur, 'Sabarimala Stand on Women and Untouchability Not the Same, Supreme Court Told', *India Today*, https://www.indiatoday.in/india/story/supreme-court-sabarimala-review-petitions-1449222-2019-02-06

35. Siddharth Prabhakar, '20 Years after Mandal, Less than 12% OBCs in Central Govt Jobs', *Times of India*, 26 December 2015, https://timesofindia.indiatimes.com/india/20-years-after-Mandal-less-than-12-OBCs-in-central-govt-jobs/articleshow/50328073.cms

36. D. Suresh Kumar, '24 Years on, OBC Workforce in Centre Still Short of Mandal Mark', *The Hindu*, 9 December 2017, https://www.thehindu.com/news/national/24-years-on-obc-workforce-in-centre-still-short-of-mandal-mark/article21382491.ece

37. Ibid.

38. Ministry of Human Resource Development, 'Strength of SCs/STs and OBCs', Public Information Bureau, 2012, https://pib.gov.in/newsite/erelcontent.aspx?relid=90995

39. Utsa Ray, 'Eating "Modernity": Changing Dietary Practices in Colonial Bengal', *Modern Asian Studies* 46.3 (2012): 703–30, http://www.jstor.org/stable/41478327

40. Brad Chase, 'Social Change at the Harappan Settlement of Gola Dhoro: A Reading from Animal Bones', *Antiquity* 84.1 (2010): 528–43, https://beef.sabhlokcity.com/Documents/beef-indus-valley-civilisation-1.pdf

41. Kancha Ilaiah Shepherd, 'Is Abrogation of Reservation on the Cards?', Wire, https://thewire.in/rights/mohan-bhagwat-rss-reservation

42. Golwalkar, *We or Our Nationhood Defined*.

43. Ibid.

Feminist Futures and Ideas of Justice for India

1. This essay is an abridged version of Kalpana Kannabiran's '"What Use Is Poetry?" Excavating Tongues of Justice around *Navtej Singh Johar vs Union of India*', *National Law School of India Review* 31.1 (2019).

2. Frantz Fanon, *Black Skin, White Masks*, trans. Charles Lam Markmann (London: Pluto Press, 2008), p. 181.

3. https://sci.gov.in/supremecourt/2016/14961/14961_2016_Judgement_06-Sep-2018.pdf

4. https://web.archive.org/web/20090826035913/http://lobis.nic.in/dhc/APS/judgement/02-07-2009/APS02072009CW74552001.pdf

5. I use 'queer' to designate all peoples who through their lives, choices and movements uproot/challenge the heteronorm. In speaking about *Johar*, likewise, I signal the large and diverse constituency of queer communities, queer rights advocates, queer persons and queer movements in the country whose incessant campaigns, petitions and determination at enormous personal and collective risk left the Supreme Court with little option but to review its stand on Section 377.

6. Leonard Zwilling and Michael J. Sweet, 'The Evolution of Third-Sex Constructs in Ancient India: A Study in Ambiguity',

in *Invented Identities: The Interplay of Gender, Religion and Politics in India*, eds. Julia Leslie and Mary McGee (New Delhi: Oxford University Press, 2000), pp. 99–132; Chayanika Shah et. al., *No Outlaws in the Gender Galaxy* (New Delhi: Zubaan, 2015).

7. For a detailed consideration of the (il)legal frameworks of surveillance and incarceration, see Kalpana Kannabiran, 'The Complexities of the Genderscape in India', *Seminar* 672 (August 2015): 46–50, and Kalpana Kannabiran, '"What Use is Poetry?" Excavating Tongues of Justice around *Navtej Singh Johar vs Union of India'*, *National Law School of India Review* 31.1 (2019). The Criminal Tribes Act (CTA), 1871 (Act XXVII of 1871 dated 12 October 1871) was subtitled 'An Act for the Registration of Criminal Tribes and Eunuchs'—the first part of the Act pertained to criminal gangs and tribes, the second part to eunuchs. Subsequently, the Criminal Tribes Act, 1911 (Act III of 1911) drops the section pertaining to 'eunuchs'. Eight years later, the Andhra Pradesh (Telangana Area) Eunuchs Act, 1329 F, an enactment of 1919 'for the registration and control of eunuchs' in the Nizam's Dominions, reproduces the provisions of the CTA for eunuchs including the forced removal of children.

8. Meena Alexander, 'What Use is Poetry?', *World Literature Today*, September 2013, https://www.worldliteraturetoday.org/2013/september/what-use-poetry-meena-alexander (emphasis added).

9. Danish Sheikh, 'Contempt', in *Global Queer Plays* (London: Oberon Books, 2018).

10. https://sci.gov.in/jonew/judis/41070.pdf

11. For a useful discussion on humiliation, see Gopal Guru, ed., *Humiliation: Claims and Context* (New Delhi: Oxford University Press, 2009).

12. Meena Alexander, 'What Use is Poetry?', *World Literature Today*.

13. K.G. Kannabiran, *The Wages of Impunity: Power, Justice and Human Rights* (Hyderabad: Orient Longman, 2003), p. 300.

14. Vaman Dada Kardak, quoted in Vaishali Vilas Sonavane, 'Lived Experiences and Cultural Renaissance: A Study of Dalit Women in Urban Employment in Maharashtra', PhD diss., (Hyderabad: Tata Institute of Social Sciences, 2018).

15. Chielozona Eze, *Ethics and Human Rights in Anglophone African Women's Literature: Feminist Empathy* (New York: Palgrave Macmillan, 2016), p. vii.

16. 'The objective of educastration is the transformation of the infant, in tendency polymorphous and "perverse", into a heterosexual adult, erotically mutilated but conforming to the Norm.' Mario Mieli, *Towards a Gay Communism: Elements of a Homosexual Critique*, trans. David Fernbach and Evan Calder Williams (London: Pluto Press, 2018), p. 4.

17. See Thomas B. Colby, 'In Defense of Judicial Empathy', *Minnesota Law Review* 96 (2012): 1982.

18. Ibid, p. 2005.

19. Stephen Breyer, interviewed by Ioanna Kohler, 'On Reading Proust', *New York Review of Books*, 7 November 2013, p. 32.

20. Mieli, *Towards a Gay Communism*, p. 2.

21. Audre Lorde, *Sister Outsider: Essays and Speeches* (Berkeley: Crossing Press, 2007), p. 113.

22. Justice Indu Malhotra, *Navtej Singh Johar vs Union of India* 17.1.

23. Justice Dhananjaya Chandrachud, *Johar*, 57 (emphasis added). In doing this, he also implicitly rejects the love–sex binary.

24. Justice Leila Seth, 'A Mother and a Judge Speak Out on Section 377', *Times of India*, 26 January 2014, quoted in Justice Chandrachud, *Johar*, 1 (emphasis added).

25. I use 'jurisprudential dissociation' to refer to 'a strategy devised by constitutional courts in India to circumvent providing critical protections to vulnerable communities against discrimination and loss of liberty, even while acknowledging in unequivocal terms, in the same case, that it was the duty of the court to protect the fundamental rights of every citizen'. Kalpana Kannabiran, *Tools of Justice: Non-Discrimination and the Indian Constitution* (New Delhi: Routledge, 2012), p. 71.

26. Kannabiran, *Tools of Justice*, pp. 444–68.

27. Upendra Baxi, 'A Constitutional Renaissance', *Indian Express,* 16 July 2018, https://indianexpress.com/article/opinion/columns/a-constitutional-renaissance-indian-judiciary-delhi-lg-powers-5260959

28. Ranajit Guha, *Elementary Aspects of Peasant Insurgency in Colonial India* (New Delhi, Oxford University Press, 1983), p. 11.

29. Kannabiran, *Wages of Impunity*.

30. Kalpana Kannabiran, 'Frontiers of Law and Society in India: Interview with Upendra Baxi', in *Selected Works of Upendra Baxi*, ed. Kalpana Kannabiran (New Delhi: Oxford University Press, forthcoming 2020).

31. *Naz Foundation vs Government of National Capital Territory (NCT) of Delhi*, 79, 104.

32. *Naz*, 99.

33. Pratap Bhanu Mehta, 'What Is Constitutional Morality?', *Seminar* 615 (2010), http://www.india-seminar.com/2010/615/615_pratap_bhanu_mehta.htm

34. B.R. Ambedkar, quoted in Chandrachud, *Johar*, 140.

35. Martha Nussbaum flattens out the complexity of this argument when she observes after *Naz*, 'The Delhi High Court has it right: laws against same-sex conduct are forms of caste hierarchy that identify a group as untouchable and stigmatize them as criminals by nature.' Martha C. Nussbaum, 'Disgust or Equality? Sexual Orientation and Indian Law', in *The Empire of Disgust: Prejudice, Discrimination, and Policy in India and the US*, eds. Zoya Hasan et al. (New Delhi: Oxford University Press, 2018), p. 194.

36. https://sci.gov.in/supremecourt/2017/19702/19702_2017_Judgement_08-Mar-2018.pdf

37. Justice Chandrachud, *Johar*, 67.

38. https://sci.gov.in/supremecourt/2006/18956/18956_2006_Judgement_28-Sep-2018.pdf

39. Justice Chandrachud, *Indian Young Lawyers Association vs the State of Kerala*, 75.

40. Savitribai Phule, quoted in Justice Chandrachud, *Indian Young Lawyers Association*, 74. In their recent work on intersectionality, Collins and Bilge foreground the figure of Savitribai Phule as someone who understood and used intersectionality without necessarily naming it as such when she 'confronted several axes of social division, namely caste, gender, religion, and economic disadvantage or class', in the course of her life and work. Patricia Hill Collins and Sirma Bilge, *Intersectionality* (Cambridge: Polity Press, 2016), p. 4.

41. Kalpana Kannabiran, 'Denying Women Entry to the Sabarimala Temple Amounts to Untouchability', Wire, 19 July 2018, https://thewire.in/law/sabarimala-temple-women-entry-supreme-court

42. Baxi, 'A Constitutional Renaissance', *Indian Express*.

43. Jack Balkin, 'The Return of Liberal Constitutionalism—And a Note on Democratic Constitutionalism', Balkinization, 31 May 2009, http://balkin.blogspot.com/2009/05/return-of-liberal-constitutionalism-and.html

44. Justice Nariman, *Justice K.S. Puttaswamy vs Union of India*, 18, https://sci.gov.in/supremecourt/2012/35071/35071_2012_Judgement_24-Aug-2017.pdf

45. Justice Chandrachud, *Johar*, 23.

46. https://sci.gov.in/supremecourt/2018/32319/32319_2018_Judgement_28-Sep-2018.pdf

47. *State of Maharashtra vs Mahesh Kariman Tirki and Others*, Sessions case no. 13 of 2014 and no. 130 of 2015, Court of Sessions Judge, Gadchiroli District, Gadchiroli.

48. See Andrew Sharpe, *Transgender Jurisprudence: Dysphoric Bodies of Law* (London: Cavendish Publishing, 2002).

49. Raewyn Connell, 'Transsexual Women and Feminist Thought: Toward New Understanding and New Politics', *Signs* 37.4 (2012): 866. Also, importantly, Mieli, *Towards a Gay Communism*.

50. Dhananjay Keer, *Dr Babasaheb Ambedkar: Life and Mission* (Mumbai: Popular Prakashan, 1990), p. 410.

Imagining and Embodying the Nation

1. Davesh Soneji, *Unfinished Gestures Devadasis, Memory, and Modernity in South India* (Chicago: University of Chicago Press, 2012), p. 122.
2. Raffaele Torella, *The Philosophical Traditions of India: An Appraisal*, trans. Kenneth F. Hurry (Varanasi: Indica Books, 2011), p. 122.
3. Ibid.
4. The list of sixteen philosophical schools includes: Charvaka, Buddhism, Jainism, Ramanuja, Purnaprajna, Pasupata, Shaivism, Pratyabhijna, Rasesvara, Vaisheshika, Nyaya, Jaimini, Paniniya, Samkhya, Patanjala and Vedanta.
5. The most popular brand of Vedanta (non-dualist) attributed to the eighth-century Adi Shankaracharya, the other main Vedanta schools being Dvaita (dualist), Vishishtadvaita and so on.

The Battle for India's Soul

1. Winston Churchill, in a speech in the House of Commons on 6 March 1947, http://hansard.millbanksystems.com/commons/1947/mar/06/india-government-policy
2. Selig S. Harrison, *India: The Most Dangerous Decades* (Princeton: Princeton University Press, 1960), p. 338.
3. 'Rate of Growth of GDP by Industry of Origin at Factor Cost & at 2004-05 Prices (Constant / Current)', Planning Commission, Government of India, http://planningcommission.nic.in/data/datatable/1203/table_17.pdf; Economic Survey of India 2010–11 and 2011–12.
4. 'Agricultural Statistics at a Glance', Department of Agriculture, Cooperation & Farmers Welfare, August 2004; Ministry of Agriculture & Farmers Welfare, 'Foodgrain Production Estimated at 257.44 MT', Press Information Bureau, 17 July 2012, https://pib.gov.in/newsite/erelease.aspx?relid=85365
5. Annual Report, Ministry of Human Resource Development, 2013–14; Economic Survey of India, 2013–14.

6. Ibid.

7. Growth of electricity sector in India from 1947–2017, Ministry of Power, Government of India, May 2017, http://www.cea.nic.in/reports/others/planning/pdm/growth_2017.pdf

8. Basic Road Statistics of India, Ministry of Road Transport and Highway, Government of India, August 2012, http://www.indiaenvironmentportal.org.in/files/file/basic%20road%20statistics%20of%20india.pdf

9. 'Selected Economy & Social Indicators (based on Economic Survey 2012-13)'.

10. Ministry of Social Justice & Empowerment, 'Baba Saheb—Emancipator of the Downtrodden', Press Information Bureau, 6 December 2006, https://pib.gov.in/newsite/erelcontent.aspx?relid=22891. Emphasis added.

11. 'Peoples' Chargesheet on Five Years of NDA Rule (2014–19)', Jan Sarokar—Peoples' Agenda, 2019.

12. 'Freedom in the World 2019: Venezuela', Freedom House, https://freedomhouse.org/report/freedom-world/2019/venezuela

13. 'Freedom in the World 2019: Philippines', Freedom House, https://freedomhouse.org/report/freedom-world/2019/philippines

14. US Department of State, '2018 Report on International Religious Freedom: Hungary', 21 June 2019, https://www.state.gov/reports/2018-report-on-international-religious-freedom/hungary

15. US Department of State, '2018 Report on International Religious Freedom: India', 21 June 2019, https://www.state.gov/reports/2018-report-on-international-religious-freedom/india/; Pushparaj V. Deshpande, 'Exclusionary Inclusion', *Economic and Political Weekly* 49.48 (November 2014).

16. Susan Hayward and Matthew J. Walton, 'Myanmar's Religious Problem: How to Deal With Discrimination', *Foreign Affairs*, 29 July 2016, https://www.foreignaffairs.com/articles/burma-myanmar/2016-07-29/myanmars-religious-problem

17. Wire, 'My Birth Is My Fatal Accident: Rohith Vemula's Searing Letter Is an Indictment of Social Prejudices', 17 January 2019, https://thewire.in/caste/rohith-vemula-letter-a-powerful-indictment-of-social-prejudices

18. Amnesty International, 'The State of the World's Human Rights 2017/18: India', 22 February 2018, https://amnesty.org.in/publications/amnesty-international-report-2017-2018-india

19. OpenDemocracy, India United Against Fascism, 'India: The BJP, Rape, and the Status of Women', 26 November 2013, https://www.opendemocracy.net/en/5050/india-bjp-rape-and-status-of-women; Mansi Sharma, 'Muzaffarnagar: Return of Gujarat memories', *India Resists*, 28 September 2013, https://indiaresists.com/muzaffarnagar-return-of-gujarat-memories/; Kavita Krishnan, 'Rape Culture and Sexism in Globalising India', *SUR* 22 (2015), https://sur.conectas.org/en/rape-culture-and-sexism-in-globalising-india

20. Jeffery Gettleman, 'An 8-Year-Old's Rape and Killing Fuels Religious Tensions in India', *New York Times*, 11 April 2018, https://www.nytimes.com/2018/04/11/world/asia/india-girl-rape.html; Mariya Salim, 'Rape as a political tool in India', Al Jazeera, 19 April 2018, https://www.aljazeera.com/indepth/opinion/rape-political-tool-india-180419091411624.html

21. Ajaz Ashraf, 'Reading Savarkar: How a Hindutva Icon Justified the Idea of Rape As a Political Tool', Scroll, 28 May 2016, https://scroll.in/article/808788/reading-savarkar-how-a-hindutva-icon-justified-the-idea-of-rape-as-a-political-tool

22. Mudasir Ahmad, 'BJP Leader in Front, Hindu Ekta Manch Waves Tricolour in Support of Rape Accused in Jammu', Wire, 17 February 2018, https://thewire.in/politics/hindu-ekta-manch-bjp-protest-support-spo-arrested-rape-jammu; Shuja-ul-Haq, 'Kathua Rape Case: 2 BJP Ministers Attend Rally in Support of Accused', *India Today*, 4 March 2018, https://www.indiatoday.in/india/story/kathua-rape-case-2-bjp-ministers-attend-rally-in-support-of-accused-1181788-2018-03-04

23. D. Mackenzie Brown, *The White Umbrella: Indian Political Thought from Manu to Gandhi* (Berkeley: University of California Press, 1953), p. 29.

24. 'Freedom in the World 2019: India', Freedom House, https://freedomhouse.org/report/freedom-world/2019/india

25. Press Trust of India, 'Unnao Gangrape Case: HC Slams UP Govt over Delay in MLA's Arrest; FIR Registered Finally', *Economic Times*, 12 April 2018, https://economictimes.indiatimes.com/news/politics-and-nation/unnao-gangrape-case-hc-slams-up-govt-over-delay-in-mlas-arrest-fir-registered-finally/articleshow/63736551.cms?from=mdr

26. Rajendra Jadhav, '5 Farmers Killed in Firing During Protest in Madhya Pradesh, Govt Orders Probe', *Livemint*, 7 June 2017, https://www.livemint.com/Politics/TmBbGSrKXJs30nqzoqb6pN/Three-protesting-farmers-shot-dead-in-Madhya-Pradesh-say-re.html; Deepak Tiwari, 'Mandsaur firing: A Year After, Where Are the 2 Probe Commissions?', *Week*, 6 June 2018, https://www.theweek.in/news/india/2018/06/06/mandsaur-firing-year-after-status-two-probe-commissions.html

27. 'Freedom in the World 2019: India', Freedom House.

28. Manuraj Shunmugasundaram, 'Towards a Southern Brotherhood', *Indian Express*, 12 April 2018, https://indianexpress.com/article/opinion/columns/towards-a-southern-brotherhood-dmk-south-india-ministers-conclave-dmk-5133622

29. '"Khan Market Gang, Lutyens Delhi Did Not Create My Image", says PM Narendra Modi in Fresh Jibe at Rahul Gandhi', *Business Today*, 12 May 2019, https://www.businesstoday.in/current/economy-politics/pm-narendra-modi-rahul-gandhi-khan-market-gang-lutyens-delhi/story/345826.html

30. Rukmini S., 'Young India Is Conservative: Opposed To Homosexuality, Likes to Marry Within Their Caste, Wants A Government Job', Huffington Post, 4 April 2017, https://www.huffingtonpost.in/2017/04/04/young-india-is-conservative-opposed-to-homosexuality-likes-to_a_22025362; 'Attitudes, Anxieties and Aspirations of India's Youth: Changing Patterns',

Centre for the Study of Developing Societies (CSDS) and Konrad Adenauer Stiftung (KAS), 3 April 2017, https://www.lokniti.org/content/CSDS-KAS-Youth-Study-2016-17

31. Dr Martin Luther King, Jr, in a speech in Chicago to protest the war in Vietnam, on 25 March 1967, https://www.jofreeman.com/photos/KingAtChicago.html

32. Pushparaj V. Deshpande, 'Reconceptualising India's Civilisational Basis', *Economic and Political Weekly* 51.39 (24 September 2016).

33. 'Tryst with Destiny Speech', Jawaharlal Nehru's address to the Constituent Assembly of India in New Delhi on 14–15 August 1947.

About the Contributors

G.N. Devy is a cultural activist known for the People's Linguistic Survey of India. He is also the founder of the Adivasi Academy, and the Bhasha Research and Publication Centre. His book *After Amnesia* (1992) is a classic in literary theory. He has published in literary criticism, anthropology, education, linguistics and philosophy.

Shashi Tharoor is member of Parliament for Thiruvananthapuram and the bestselling author of nineteen books, most recently *The Hindu Way*. He was undersecretary-general of the United Nations, and minister of state for human resource development, and for external affairs, Government of India. He has won numerous awards, including the Pravasi Bharatiya Samman and the Commonwealth Writers' Prize.

Neera Chandhoke is former professor of political science, University of Delhi. Her latest book is *Rethinking Pluralism, Secularism, and Tolerance: Anxieties of Coexistence* (2019). She has written on democracy, secession and civil society, and is published in national and international journals. Her current work is on political violence in India.

Sitaram Yechury is general secretary of the Communist Party of India (Marxist) and a member of the Politburo of the Communist Party of India (Marxist). He was the party's parliamentary group leader, and a two-term member of Parliament (Rajya Sabha).

S.Y. Quraishi is a former IAS officer. He was the chief election commissioner of India, as well as secretary in the Ministry of Youth Affairs and Sports. He has authored two books, *An Undocumented Wonder: The Making of the Great Indian Election* and *Old Delhi: Living Traditions*.

Syeda Hameed is a former member of the Planning Commission of India, and the National Commission for Women. A recipient of the Padma Shri, Hameed chaired the Steering Committee of the Commission on Health, and is founder-trustee of the Women's Initiative for Peace in South Asia, and the Centre for Dialogue and Reconciliation.

Kancha Ilaiah Shepherd is director, Centre for Social Exclusion and Inclusive Policy at Maulana Azad National Urdu University, Hyderabad. A recipient of the Mahatma Jyotirao Phule Award, he has been a member of the National Research Committee, Ministry of Social Justice. Among his influential books are *Why I Am Not a Hindu* (1996) and *Buffalo Nationalism* (2004).

Kalpana Kannabiran is professor and director, Council for Social Development, Hyderabad. She is recipient of the Amartya Sen Award and the VKRV Rao Prize. She was a founding faculty of NALSAR University, and of Asmita Resource Centre for Women. She works on constitutionalism and social justice, especially gender, sexual minorities, caste, Adivasi rights and disability rights.

Navtej Singh Johar is a dancer–choreographer, scholar, yoga exponent and social activist. His work remains body-centric, twining practice with critical theory and social action. The director of Studio Abhyas, New Delhi, he has devised two new systems of embodied practice: the BARPS method as well as Abhyas Somatics (www.abhyastrust.org).

Pushparaj Deshpande is the director of the Samruddha Bharat Foundation. He has worked on legislation, policy and strategy with various legislators, a think tank, a political consultancy, a media channel and a national political party. He writes columns for diverse publications.